ENCOURAGE
READING
FROM THE START

ALA Editions purchases fund advocacy, awareness,
and accreditation programs for library professionals worldwide.

ENCOURAGE READING

FROM THE START

essays, articles, and interviews from the field

PAT R. SCALES

ala editions

An imprint of the American Library Association
Chicago 2018

PAT SCALES is a 1966 graduate of the University of Montevallo (AL), and received a MLS from George Peabody College for Teachers of Vanderbilt University in 1972. She served as librarian at Greenville Middle School for twenty-six years and was the first Director of Library Services at the South Carolina Governors School for the Arts and Humanities. She taught children's and young adult literature for twenty-seven years at Furman University, and has taught special topics courses at the University of Texas, Louisiana State University, Drexel University, and University of South Carolina. She is a past President of the Association for Library Service to Children, a division of the American Library Association, and has served as chair of the prestigious Newbery, Caldecott, and Wilder Award Committees. Scales has been actively involved with ALA's Intellectual Freedom Committee for a number of years, and served two terms as chair. She is a member of the Freedom to Read Foundation, serves on the Council of Advisers of the National Coalition Against Censorship, and acts as a spokesperson for first amendment issues as they relate to children and young adults. She is the author of *Teaching Banned Books: Twelve Guides for Young Readers*, *Protecting Intellectual Freedom in Your School Library*, *Books Under Fire: A Hit List of Banned and Challenged Children's Books*, *Defending Frequently Challenged Young Adult Books*, and *Scales on Censorship: Real Life Lessons from School Library Journal*. She writes a bimonthly column, "Scales on Censorship," for *School Library Journal*, curriculum guides on children's and young adult books for a number of publishers, and is a regular contributor to *Book Links* magazine.

© 2018 by the American Library Association

Extensive effort has gone into ensuring the reliability of the information in this book; however, the publisher makes no warranty, express or implied, with respect to the material contained herein.

ISBN 978-0-8389-1650-6 (paper)

Library of Congress Cataloging-in-Publication Data
Names: Scales, Pat R., author.
Title: Encourage reading from the start : essays, articles, and interviews
  from the field / Pat R. Scales.
Description: First edition. | Chicago : ALA Editions, an imprint of the
  American Library Association, 2018. | "A Booklist publication." | The
  articles, essays and interviews included in this volume are a selection of
  the author's contributions to Book Links magazine. | Includes
  bibliographical references and index.
Identifiers: LCCN 2017031638 | ISBN 9780838916506 (pbk. : alk. paper)
Subjects: LCSH: Children--Books and reading—United States. | Reading
  promotion—United States. | Reading, Psychology of. | Children's
  libraries—Activity programs—United States. | School libraries—Activity
  programs—United States. | Authors, American—Interviews. | Children's
  literature, American—Bibliography. | Young adult literature,
  American—Bibliography.
Classification: LCC Z1037.A1 S263 2018 | DDC 028.5/5—dc23 LC record available at https://
lccn.loc.gov/2017031638

⊚ This paper meets the requirements of ANSI/NISO Z39.48–1992 (Permanence of Paper).

Printed in the United States of America

22 21 20 19 18   5 4 3 2 1

This book is for

Barbara Elleman

Laura Tillotson

and

Gillian Engberg

What a Great Journey It Has Been!
Your Vision and Creativity Are Unmatched

CONTENTS

Preface / ix

PART 1: HOW READING SHAPES US — 1

Playing House 3

Talking with Elana K. Arnold 6

Somewhere in the Darkness 16

Gotcha Day 21

Talking with Rita Williams-Garcia 24

Let's Read Short Shorts 35

Sidetracked by Books 39

Reading Turquoise 41

Ambassador of the World 44

PART 2: WHAT HISTORY TELLS US — 47

Moving Day 49

How Do We Say Thank You, Jean Fritz?. 52

Jean Fritz's You Want Women to Vote, Lizzie Stanton?. . .55

Talking with Gennifer Choldenko. 64

It's Not My War 70

Talking with Graham Salisbury. 72

They Laughed 82

Talking with Angela Cerrito. 85

No One Wanted Us. 94

Talking with Susan Goldman Rubin. 97

Loving v. Virginia and Interracial Families 109

Trouble, Folks. 115

PART 3: WHERE SCIENCE LEADS US   119

The Man in the Moon 121

My Mother Was Rosie the Riveter 125

Talking with Steve Sheinkin. 128

Architecture and Construction. .135

On the Street Where I Lived. 141

Families Coping with Mental Illness. 144

PART 4: WHEN ART INSPIRES US   151

A Lesson from Frank 153

E. L. Konigsburg's *The Second
Mrs. Giaconda:* An Update. 156

"Pointe" the Way. 163

Times a-Changin'. 166

PART 5: HOW FREEDOM TO READ DEFINES US   169

It's About Conversation. 171

Studying the First Amendment .175

Because of Alice: Phyllis Reynolds Naylor's Alice Books. . .186

Talking with Dori Hillestad Butler. 193

Three Bombs, Two Lips, and a Martini Glass 200

It's September 204

Index / 207

PREFACE

The articles, essays, and interviews included in this volume are a collection of my contributions to *Book Links* magazine, which is a *Booklist* publication. *Book Links* was Barbara Elleman's brainchild, and I still remember her enthusiasm about serving school and public librarians and classroom teachers by creating a unique publication to "connect children with high-quality literature-based resources." She and I sat in a hotel room in New Orleans and talked about her vision, planning the first issue of the magazine. She asked me to write a regular column called "Book Strategies"; the idea was to highlight one book and draw connections between the topics and themes in that novel with other fiction and nonfiction, in a combination of front- and backlist titles. There would also be ideas for classroom discussion and activities that encouraged creative and critical thought. That was in 1990, and I'm thrilled to have been a part of the magazine since the very first issue.

My first column featured *The Second Mrs. Giaconda* (1978) by E. L. Konigsburg. I had used the book very successfully with middle-school students, and I knew that it was easy to generate interest in Leonardo da Vinci. It was a perfect selection to connect language arts, science, social studies, and art. Neither Barbara nor I ever considered the fact that the book was out of print. The magazine was printed and circulated, and I got a call from E. L. Konigsburg, who said that *Book Links* had just accomplished something she had been trying to do for years: the book had been brought back into print.

The article was reprinted in the tenth anniversary issue of *Book Links,* and is included in this volume. Today, Konigsburg's novel is available in e-book format, and the "Book Strategies" feature remains relevant.

A lot has happened in education since the early days of *Book Links.* The nation has been through a number of attempts to reform education. The Clinton administration reauthorized the Elementary Secondary Education Act, which morphed into the Bush administration's No Child Left Behind. Now, the Common Core State Standards have aroused so much political opposition that most states have withdrawn endorsement of them. No one can possibly predict what road the U.S. Department of Education may take next. But the truth of the matter is that, though educational standards adopt new names, good teaching remains the same. And *Book Links* continues to support and celebrate the commitment of librarians and teachers as they lead their students to think, create, and connect knowledge from across the curriculum, regardless of what those standards are called.

Currently, the magazine is published quarterly as a *Booklist* supplement. Each issue is devoted to one curriculum area, but the original mission of making connections through literature remains. There are interviews with writers and illustrators, and topical classroom connections aimed at students from preschool age through the eighth grade. Laura Tillotson came to *Book Links* from her post as a children's book editor at Farrar, Straus and Giroux. It was her idea to include a back-page essay, which she asked me to write. I can still hear her laughter when she received the first "Weighing In" column, called "RIP, Dracula," inspired by my seventh-grade science teacher, who knew very little about teaching science.

Each of the editors of *Book Links* worked with advisory boards and attended professional conferences to find out exactly what professionals expected from the publication. And they called upon their own creative genius to put their special stamp on the magazine. Gillian Engberg, who followed Laura, is to be lauded for being nimble as *Book Links* revamped its structure.

Booklist editor Bill Ott suggested that my columns be anthologized. As I began looking at the articles I have written since the very first issue of *Book Links,* it became apparent that there are simply too many pieces to include in one volume. I have selected thirty-six for *Encourage Reading from the Start.*

The book is divided into five parts: "How Reading Shapes Us," "What History Tells Us," "Where Science Leads Us," "When Art Inspires Us," and "How Freedom to Read Defines Us." Each section includes subject-appropriate feature articles, interviews with writers, and essays chosen from the "Weighing In" columns. One of the essays in the last section was originally published in *Booklist,* and another in *Knowledge Quest,* a publication of the American Association of School Librarians.

It should be noted that the inconsistencies in the way the feature articles and interviews are presented represent the editorial changes in *Book Links* since its inception. Each entry includes the date it appeared in the magazine. Out-of-print (o.p.) books have traditionally been included in the bibliographies, but it is likely that some books that were in print at the time some articles were written are out of print now. The titles remain relevant, though, since libraries are filled with out-of-print books that are vital to the classroom curriculum, or to accommodate reader interests.

There were no suggested grade levels for featured and related books in the early issues of *Book Links,* but somewhere along the way grade levels for each book entry were added. Too many librarians and teachers confuse grade level with actual reading level, however. For this reason, I have taken the liberty to remove the suggested grade levels. The bibliographic information and the annotations for each entry are a clue to the targeted audience.

In recent years, *Book Links* has aligned its book activities with Common Core State Standards. Questions for book discussions and suggestions for classroom activities are included, but all references to the state standards have been removed. Some articles provide a link to an extensive Educator's Guide located on the publisher's website.

From the very beginning, *Book Links* has been an invaluable resource for teachers and school librarians. I want to make a case for its use in public libraries as well. School districts without strong school libraries turn to public libraries for guidance as they develop units of study for students. They want to know fiction and nonfiction works that support and enhance the topics covered in textbooks. Often children's and teen librarians go to schools to tell readers about books, and to introduce them to writers that may interest them. And parents and their children look to public libraries as a resource for homework help. The questions for book discussion, and even some of the extension activities, are extremely useful for book clubs. Public librarians are encouraged to select the features that best serve the needs of young patrons and the parents, teachers, and school librarians who work with them each and every day.

I wish that I had had *Book Links* as a resource when I began my career as a school librarian forty-six years ago. There was no publication that mirrored what *Book Links* offers, but I was fortunate to have children's literature professors, in undergraduate and graduate school, who stressed the importance of helping children make the all-important connection between books of similar topics and themes to broaden their knowledge and expand their reading interests. These professors believed that this was the only way to teach children to think creatively and critically, and to eventually take responsibility for their own guided reading as they matured into literate adults. It was these professors' philosophy that shaped my professional beliefs as I worked daily to excite children about books, and to guide their teachers in using children's books to enhance the curriculum for which they were responsible.

It has been a great journey with *Book Links,* and I sincerely hope that this anthology inspires all professionals who work with children and books.

PART 1

HOW READING SHAPES US

"It's important to offer readers novels that mirror the kinds of families in which they live. At the same time, stories about all types of families help children develop empathy."

PLAYING HOUSE

**ery large pine trees surrounded the playground at my** elementary school. We had recess, instead of physical education, at which time the boys would scatter to a nearby open field for a pickup game of baseball, and the girls would jump rope or play house under the branches of the trees. Pine needles were perfect to outline the rooms of our imaginary houses, and the giant roots served as furniture. In our game of house, the fathers were always away at work and returned home in time for dinner. The mothers were content to cook, clean, and take care of the children. It never dawned on most of us that any other family structure existed because we were products of traditional homes, in which the family—a father, a mother, and several children—shared the supper table every night. I did know a few kids with no father in the home, but it never occurred to me to question why.

Twenty years later, I took my niece to a city park to play. There was a group of girls using the jungle gym as an imaginary house. The squares created by the bars formed the rooms. One girl appointed herself the mother and instructed the others to be her children. Not quite satisfied with the bossy mother, one of the children asked, "Who is the daddy?" The mother replied, "There's not a daddy in our house." It was at this moment that I realized that a playhouse of the late 1970s was vastly different from the ones my friends and I created on the school playground in the 1950s. In the decades that followed, the concept of family has been redefined many times. Children may live with one parent, a grandmother, or another relative. The family may include two mothers or two fathers. It may be biracial or bicultural. Yet this doesn't mean that children aren't loved within their family unit, regardless of what that family looks like.

Many social and economic factors impact families today. It's important to offer readers novels that mirror the kinds of families in which they live. At the same time, stories about all types

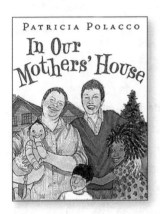

of families help children develop empathy. It's very likely that most schools have students who have same-sex parents. *In Our Mothers' House,* by Patricia Polacco, reveals the love and keen sense of family that exists in a house with two mothers. A mixed-race boy is sent to New Orleans to finally meet his dead father's family in *Zane and the Hurricane,* by Rodman Philbrick. He gets to know his grandmother and a whole lot of other people as they struggle to survive Hurricane Katrina. In *One Crazy Summer,* by Rita Williams-Garcia, three sisters spend a month with their mother, who abandoned them in search of her own brand of happiness. Back home, their father and grandmother eagerly await their return. Phyllis Reynolds Naylor shows what happens when a girl from Appalachia and a wealthy city girl learn to appreciate one another after spending time together in *Faith, Hope and Ivy June.* Carl Hiaasen leaves a boy whose mother is out of the country on business in charge of his erratic dad in *Chomp. Al Capone Does My Shirts,* by Gennifer Choldenko, reveals how a special-needs child affects the daily lives of an entire family, especially when they are isolated by their life on Alcatraz.

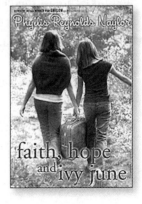

Some families, such as the one in *The Mighty Miss Malone,* by Christopher Paul Curtis, are torn apart by homelessness. Others live under a cloud of mental illness, as in *Sure Signs of Crazy,* by Karen Harrington. And many of the loneliest children are those who go home to nannies and babysitters while their parents travel Europe or spend late nights at the office chasing success. These children are sure to identify with Harriet Welsch in Louise Fitzhugh's *Harriet the Spy.*

At the beginning of the academic year, some school districts send teachers on a school-bus tour of the neighborhoods where their students live. In some neighborhoods, they see dilapidated houses with no heat or air conditioning. In other areas, they see abandoned cars in which entire families are living. They also see large homes with pools and tennis courts in the backyards and luxury apartment buildings. These sharp contrasts in families and the way they live shape the culture of our nation's classrooms. How do all of these children play house? What do their imaginary families look like? It's for sure that there are children's books to support their definition of family.

January 2014

TALKING WITH
ELANA K. ARNOLD

outhern California and the Pacific Northwest may not seem far apart to some, but they might as well be separate countries for two of Elana K. Arnold's protagonists: Iris Abernathy (*The Question of Miracles,* 2015) and Odette Zyskowski (*Far from Fair,* 2016). Each girl is forced to leave her school and friends, and each, readers learn, is dealing with some kind of grief.

Iris, an only child, moves when her mother takes a new job in Oregon. Her dad maintains the house and makes plans to plant a garden and raise chick-

ens. Boris, a seemingly odd boy at school, befriends Iris and explains that he is, medically speaking, a miracle child. He thinks the house where the Abernathys live resembles a haunted mansion, and convinces Iris that the sound she hears from her closet may indeed be the voice of her friend Sarah, who died just before the Abernathys moved. He even encourages her to visit a psychic to help her make a connection with Sarah. Why couldn't there have been a miracle for Sarah? Iris' parents sense that

she is still struggling with Sarah's death, and they
send her to a therapist. The journey is tough, but
the sprouting of new plants and the hatching of the
eggs her father has nurtured represents new life and
serves as a symbol of hope for Iris.

Odette's situation is more complicated. Her
parents have hidden their troubled marriage, but
it becomes obvious when the family sets out for
Orcas Island, off the coast of Washington, in a used
RV. They sold most of their belongings when they
vacated their home, and now Odette, her autis-
tic brother, and their parents live in cramped quarters with only one cell
phone between them. Odette makes several observations upon arrival on the
island. Grandma Sissy's bakery is dark, and the apartment above it where
her grandmother lives is aglow with light. She knew that her grandmother
had been sick, but she didn't realize until now that Grandma Sissy wasn't
going to get better. Then Odette learns that Washington is a right-to-die state
and Grandma Sissy has elected to determine her time to die. When that day
comes, the family holds Grandma Sissy's memorial service in her bakery. It's
not without hope: Odette's family is able to take over the bakery and begin
a new chapter in their lives.

Quiet and almost old-fashioned in tone, *Far from Fair* and *The Question of
Miracles* each tackle tough issues for a younger audience; Arnold offers hope
as she asks readers to ponder some of life's biggest struggles. In the following
conversation, she discusses not only these two titles but also the depictions
of death, grief, and recovery in her novels and how such depictions change
when writing for a younger audience.

SCALES: *The Question of Miracles* and *Far from
Fair* **have characters that move to the Pacific
Northwest. Why are you so drawn to this set-
ting?**

ARNOLD: In 2009, my husband and I—for complicated reasons—sold our beautiful southern

California '50s ranch-style home and moved our two small children, our dog, Sherman, and our illegal ferret, Vegas, into an old RV, beginning a journey up the coast of California and toward an uncertain future

Before getting in the Coach, as we called it, life hadn't been perfect. There was the enormous mortgage we really couldn't afford, which I wrestled with each month, trying to do magic math to make our money stretch in ways it really couldn't; there was my husband's regular disappearance into the garage to smoke cigars and ruminate on the stresses of his work; there was the tension in our marriage, fed by all of the above. So when he came home from work one day, wild-eyed and nervous, and said, "I got laid off today," we chose to try something different. We sold it all—at an enormous loss— and drove away.

On the road north, I started writing again for the first time in many years. I had a blog—*People Do Things*—about our travels, our hopes, my fears. I had time to write without the house and the chores, without laundry to wash or dishes to do.

When we pulled into Corvallis, Oregon, not too many months later, it felt like a town that could be our home. We parked the RV in the driveway of a rented house on Roseberry Lane. The kids found friends. I found a job teaching at Oregon State University. My husband stayed home for the first time in our kids' lives and found he was pretty good at being a stay-at-home dad.

It sounds like the end of a book, but I've learned from writing and from life that a structurally satisfying ending usually isn't where things stay put.

We didn't stay in Corvallis, Oregon, for very long—just under a year—but the Pacific Northwest has stayed with me. The time we spent there, though some of it quite hard, was important. The rainstorms, the constant wetness, and the many shades of green followed me home to southern California. I visit them in my writing.

SCALES: Iris Abernathy, the main character in *The Question of Miracles,* and Odette Zyskowski, the main character in *Far from Fair,* are dealing with grief. You have also written young adult books that deal with grief. Tell us about your journey to explore this theme for middle and young adult readers.

ARNOLD: When we were living in Corvallis, Oregon, our favorite place to eat was American Dream Pizza. One day, all tucked in and cozy in a booth, a beautiful pizza in front of us, feeling happy and celebratory and fine, I got a call from my sister back home in California. She called to tell me that my best friend from high school had killed herself that afternoon. My first response was, "But she'll be okay, right?" It was too much to believe that the girl I loved so much, who was so full of life and smarts and ambition, was all the way dead. I wanted for her to at least be a little bit alive.

Less than a year after her death, I began writing my first novel, *Sacred* (2012), a book about a girl dealing with a sudden, unexpected death. And I have written about death many times since then. Death is something that bothers me, a lot. I'm afraid of dying, but even more than that, I love living so very much that the knowledge that life must end—my own life, the lives of those I love, and my children's lives, most of all—is almost impossible to bear. So I return again and again to the questions of death and how one lives a meaningful life in spite of death and grief.

SCALES: In *Far from Fair,* you deal with the right to die with incredible grace. At what point in writing the novel did you know you wanted to tackle this important issue?

ARNOLD: When I began writing *Far from Fair,* I imagined it as a road trip story about a family jammed together in a broken-down, old RV. The family was going to travel across the country, visiting the parents' parents and stepparents. It was going to be light and funny and without death. But like a road trip, novel writing sometimes takes turns one can't anticipate. About 60 pages into the first draft, I realized that when my characters got to Grandma Sissy's house, they were going to find a terminally ill woman, and they were all going to have to deal with questions about mortality and the right to die.

But now, looking back, it seems so obvious that this would be where the book would head; in the midst of writing the book, I was driving with my dad to his weekly appointments at the City of Hope, a cancer hospital, and talking with him about the end of his life and how he hoped to face it.

My dad lived until after I finished writing *Far from Fair,* and he read an early draft. He was proud of the book, and he was proud of me.

SCALES: Odette is confused by her parents' relationship in *Far from Fair,* and her autistic brother adds to the strained interaction between all members of the family. Take us through the creation of this complicated family.

ARNOLD: There are elements of this family that mirror my own family, and parts of it are entirely fictional. What always surprises me is when my own self seeps into my work in ways I didn't intend. I don't see these places clearly until I've taken a step back, usually during the revision process. This is true of Odette's parents' marriage. During the first draft, there was no concrete mention of their troubles, but when I dug back in, I saw the strain and tension between them and recognized it as a reflection of the difficulties my husband and I had encountered during our overextended years. As I revised in conjunction with my wonderful editor at Houghton Mifflin Harcourt—and there were many drafts—the marriage problems became clearer to me, more on-the-page in a way that strengthens the book. All the family dynamics became more complicated, and Odette's central complaint—that things just aren't fair—became louder, too.

SCALES: Iris has a stay-at-home dad in *The Question of Miracles.* Did you set out to write a book that addresses the changing gender roles in our society, or did it happen naturally?

ARNOLD: I didn't set out to write a book that addressed anything in particular. I had a character—Iris—who I knew was deeply sad and lonely, and I knew she and her family had moved to a new town. The family unfolded for me very much as they unfold for the reader. Of course, with some distance, I see the many ways Iris' family mirrors my own, but when I was writing, I didn't see the similarities.

SCALES: Do you believe in miracles?

ARNOLD: Yes. No. I don't know.

SCALES: Light and darkness are presented in different forms in your novels. Why is it so important for young readers to see both lightness and darkness in novels?

ARNOLD: Maybe not during my earliest years, but definitely as long as my memory reaches, I have been careful to soak up the things that bring me joy—the sweet citrus scent of an orange just peeled; the warm weight of a lapful of sleeping cat; the anticipation of coffee nearly made. I notice and enjoy these things because one day I will die. The awareness of death—that human recognition of mortality—does it enable us to engage more fully in the time and experiences we do have than if we were ignorant of our inevitable end? I think so. Light and dark—life and death—are with us every day, whether we speak of them or not. I think it's comforting and empowering for readers of all ages to confront the various ways lightness and darkness exist in our everyday lives.

SCALES: How is writing middle-grade fiction different from writing for young adults?

ARNOLD: I like to say that I write books *for* kids and books *about* teens. When I am working on a YA project, I do my very best to ignore my hope that one day the book will find an audience. I write the book that pleases and challenges me, and I follow the story wherever it goes. When I write for younger people—middle-graders and children—I do consider my audience. Of the two, I find writing books for kids to be much more pleasurable than writing about teens, but I am grateful that I am able to follow the stories that come to me, and that no one has tried to brand me as one kind of writer.

SCALES: Which of your characters is most like you?

ARNOLD: There's a famous belief that first novels are thinly veiled autobiographies. My first book, *Sacred,* set on Catalina Island, off the coast of California, tells the story of Scarlett Wenderoth, a lonely, bookish teen whose brother dies, and who meets a mysterious newcomer to the island who may be a kabbalah mystic (spoiler alert: he is). I have never lived on an island, and I have never lost a sibling, and I have never (yet) fallen in love with a kabbalah mystic. So I felt smugly certain that I had avoided the novel-as-autobiography trap, until I reread my book after some time had passed, after it was published. Suddenly, I saw myself as a teen—the way I felt about my body, the way I felt about boys and friends and parents and horses—and it was brutally clear that I had laid myself bare on the page, even though the plot was fictional. That said, I know I am in all of my characters—the teens, the kids, and the grown-ups, too. In fact, Claude, a psychic that Iris visits in

The Question of Miracles, tells a story of her first, heartbreaking friendship that I lived word-for-word.

SCALES: Tell us about some of the books you remember most from your childhood.

ARNOLD: I loved *Bridge to Terabithia, From the Mixed-up Files of Mrs. Basil E. Frankweiler,* and *Harriet the Spy.* I didn't think about it at the time, but now I see that all three of these books feature girls who love to read and whose reading inspires them to take real-life chances, whether that means building an imaginary world, running away from home to live in a museum, or spying on the neighbors. When I was a little older, *Anne of Green Gables* absolutely captured me. I wanted to BE Anne. The Halloween of my seventh-grade year, I tried to dye my hair red with a bottle of food coloring and ended up with weird pink stripes that lasted until New Year's.

SCALES: Have any of these titles inspired your writings?

ARNOLD: Absolutely, all of them have influenced my writing. I liked the everydayness of these books, how magic happens in the ordinary. I liked the connections between realistic characters; I liked the imperfect but not ridiculous parents; I liked how the smallest shifts in dialogue, plot, and mood could create seismic transformations in how the characters saw themselves and those around them. Both *The Question of Miracles* and *Far from Fair* work in this tradition of "quiet," realistic books.

SCALES: What questions do you get from your readers? Have any of their letters inspired ideas for other novels?

ARNOLD: The most common questions I get are about the endings of *Splendor* (2013, *Sacred*'s sequel) and *Burning* (2013). These stories, though romantic, are not romances, and as such, don't make any happily-ever-after promises. I get letters from readers asking me to tell them more, asking me to say that yes, eventually, the characters do decide on a lifetime with each other. I get asked for sequels to these books, but for me the endings feel perfect just as they are. So far, I haven't gotten any inspiration for new novels, but I am open to the possibility!

SCALES: What are you writing now?

ARNOLD: I just finished the final edits of *A Boy Called BAT* and am working on its sequel! This is the official description: "In the spirit of Clementine and Ramona, the books follow Bixby Alexander Tam—nicknamed BAT—a third-grader on the autism spectrum, and his funny, authentic experiences at home and at school." I love BAT, as I love Iris and Odette, and I am deeply grateful for each reader, child and adult, who loves these characters, too.

SAMPLING ARNOLD

Burning. 2013. Delacorte, e-book, $9.99 (9780375991080).

Far from Fair. 2016. HMH, $16.99 (9780544602274).

Infandous. 2015. Carolrhoda/Lab, $18.99 (9781467738491).

The Question of Miracles. 2015. HMH, $16.99 (9780544334649).

Sacred. 2012. Delacorte, $17.99 (9780385742115).

Splendor. 2013. Delacorte, $17.99 (9780385742139).

FURTHER READING

The following titles about children coping with grief, often after a tragedy within their own families, make excellent companions to *The Question of Miracles* and *Far from Fair.*

Bridge to Terabithia. By Katherine Paterson. 1977. HarperCollins, $16.99 (9780690013597).

> In this Newbery award novel, Jess Aarons becomes friends with a new girl in town, and the two create an imaginary kingdom they call Terabithia. When Leslie drowns while crossing the creek to Terabithia, Jess struggles to deal with his loss.

Finding the Worm. By Mark Goldblatt. 2015. Random, $16.99 (9780385391085).

> In this sequel to *Twerp* (2013), seventh-grader Julian Twerski and his friends are up to their usual mischief, but when their friend Quentin is diagnosed with cancer, the kids are suddenly faced with hard questions about life and death.

The Fourteenth Goldfish. By Jennifer L. Holm. 2014. Random, $19.99 (9780375970641).

> Middle school is tough for 11-year-old Ellie after she and her best friend part ways. Things look up for her when her grandfather, a scientist, moves

in and helps her contemplate tough issues and navigate the many changes in her life.

Kira-Kira. **By Cynthia Kadohata. 2004. Atheneum, $17.99 (9780689856396).**
Katie's family moves from Iowa to a small town in Georgia to work alongside other Japanese Americans in the chicken business. The family is devastated when Lynn, the older daughter, dies of leukemia and they have little money to pay the medical bills.

Missing May. **By Cynthia Rylant. 1992. Orchard/Richard Jackson, $15.99 (9780439613835).**
Summer, an orphan, has finally found a loving home with Aunt May and Uncle Ob deep in the heart of Appalachia, and when May dies, Summer and her uncle are overcome with grief. Then they take a road trip together, and the two learn to celebrate May's life by sharing special memories of her.

Nest. **By Esther Ehrlich. 2014. Random/Wendy Lamb, $16.99 (9780385386074).**
Naomi "Chirp" Orenstein's family is turned upside down when her mother, a dancer, falls into a deep depression after being diagnosed with multiple sclerosis and ultimately commits suicide. Joey, a neighbor who is abused by his father, seems to understand Chirp's sadness.

The Thing about Jellyfish. **By Ali Benjamin. 2015. Little, Brown, $17 (9780316380867).**
Suzy is sad about the fight that she and Franny Jackson, a longtime best friend, had months before their seventh-grade year. When Franny drowns, Suzy must find ways to deal with the many layers of grief.

The Watsons Go to Birmingham—1963. **By Christopher Paul Curtis. Delacorte, $16.95 (9780385321754).**
The Watsons set out on a long trip from Flint, Michigan, to Birmingham, Alabama, to deliver Byron, the oldest son, to his grandmother for some strict discipline because he bullies his younger brother, Kenny. They travel through the Jim Crow South and witness the bombing of the Sixteenth Baptist Church, which turns out to be a life-changing moment for all of the Watsons, especially Byron and Kenny.

IN THE CLASSROOM

- Iris Abernathy, the main character in *The Question of Miracles,* and Odette Zyskowski, the main character in *Far from Fair,* move from California to the Pacific Northwest. Allow students to work as partners and have them each take the role of one of the main characters. Then instruct them to exchange letters about the difficulties of adjusting to their move, making new friends, and so on.

- Engage readers in a discussion about the family issues in the two novels. Contrast Iris' and Odette's parents: How are the girls' relationships with their respective fathers? How are their mothers strong in different ways? You can expand the discussion into the ways each family finds hope, by discussing the following quote from *The Question of Miracles:* "But hoping, Iris decided, is not the same as knowing" (p.230). What is the difference in knowing and hoping? How do these family relationships fit in?

- Iris is dealing with the sudden death of a friend, and Odette is facing the death of Grandma Sissy after a battle with cancer. Ask students to read another novel, from the suggested list or elsewhere, where the main character is dealing with death. Have them write a brief paper that compares this loss to those of Iris or Odette. Encourage students to cite specific passages from the books to support their thoughts.

- Grandma Sissy is terminally ill and by law is allowed Death with Dignity. Read about the Death with Dignity Act on the following website: https://www.deathwithdignity.org/learn/access/. What are the guidelines that doctors and patients must follow? The right to die has created heated debates in some states. Older students may wish to engage in a debate about this issue.

April 2016

SOMEWHERE IN THE DARKNESS

BY WALTER DEAN MYERS

n celebration of 25 years of *Book Links,* we are taking another look at articles from earlier issues. Pat Scales' examination of father-son relationships in Walter Dean Myers' Newbery Honor Book, *Somewhere in the Darkness,* originally ran in our March 1993 issue.

In this award-winning book, Myers weaves an emotionally charged story filled with questions regarding relationships, right and wrong, love and anger, and the importance of truth. This intimate and heart-wrenching young adult novel presents a 15-year-old protagonist who is reunited with his father after years of separation. Jimmy Little knows almost nothing about his father except that he is in prison for committing murder. Since his mother's death, Jimmy has lived with his aunt in her small fourth-floor apartment in a seventh-story building in the heart of Harlem. Though his inner-city environment has made him streetwise, Jimmy, under the watchful eye of Mama Jean, leads a clean life and manages to mind his own business and stay out of trouble. Daydreaming and skipping school are his only real problems. But one day, when he comes home from school and finds a strange man claiming to be his father, Jimmy faces some hard truths: What crime did his father commit? Why is he suddenly out of jail? What does he want from Jimmy?

Jimmy often daydreamed about his father and what little Mama Jean had told him regarding his father's crime—"There had been a holdup, and some men had been killed"—but the harsh details of his dad's criminal act had been left to his imagination. Now, a critically ill man calling himself Crab Little is standing in Mama Jean's apartment, announcing that he has been paroled and has plans for Jimmy: "I thought you and me might go around the country a bit. . . . I need to have a family for a while." Mama Jean has been Jimmy's family, providing him with

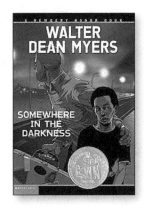

love, compassion, and understanding, but Crab's need to "make things right" with his son and Jimmy's daydreams about having a father win over Mama Jean's protest, and the two embark on a trip that takes them from New York to Chicago and finally to Arkansas, Crab's boyhood home.

Throughout the trip, Jimmy silently questions Crab. How did his father afford to buy a car? Where did Crab get the wad of money that he has in his pocket? Why do they have to stop so often and make telephone calls? Who is Rydell and why is it so important for Crab to find him? When Jimmy sees his father use a credit card with someone else's name on it, he begins to find the answers to some of his questions. He realizes that Crab's life is filled with lies and dishonest dealings. He discovers that his father is not on parole, but has broken out of the prison hospital with the purpose of finding his son and proving to him that he didn't commit murder. And he comes to grips with the hardest truth of all: Crab can never be the father of his daydreams—a man who will take him to baseball games or for a walk in the park.

When Jimmy and his father reach Marion, Arkansas, Crab seeks out Rydell, the only man who knows the truth about his crime. "I brought my boy here so he could hear the truth. . . . And I mean for him to hear it." But Rydell doesn't trust Crab, and refuses to talk. In a moment of truth, Jimmy finally says to his father, "It don't make a difference if you didn't kill anybody. . . . Not if you're going to steal some money or credit cards or something. That's wrong too. It don't make you good just because you didn't kill nobody."

In a dramatic end to their journey, Crab collapses in pain upon being captured by the police. He is taken to a hospital, where he eventually dies with

Jimmy at his side. Though father and son never really reconcile the "truth," the reunion does shape Jimmy's idea of the kind of father that he wants to be. During the train ride back to New York and the security of Mama Jean's home, Jimmy dreams about having a son. "He would tell him all the secrets he knew, looking right into his eyes and telling him nothing but the truth so that every time they were together they would know things about each other."

FATHERS AND SONS

The following titles, updated since the original 1993 publication of this article, include more current works dealing with father-son relationships.

Bang. By Sharon Flake. 2007. Hyperion, $8.99 (9780786849550).
> A father who is grieving the senseless death of his younger son turns his older son out in the streets to teach him about becoming a man.

Bud, Not Buddy. By Christopher Paul Curtis. 1999. Delacorte, $16.99 (9780385323062).
> Set during the Great Depression, Bud, a 10-year-old foster child, sets out to find his father but, instead, stumbles upon his grandfather.

Mariposa Blues. By Ronald Koertge. 1991. Harper, $3.50 (9780380717613).
> The summer at Mariposa Downs turns out to be a time of change for 13-year-old Graham, who finds himself questioning his relationship with his father while searching for his own identity.

Sons from Afar. By Cynthia Voigt. 2012. Simon & Schuster, $18.99 (9781442450653).
> James and Sammy Tillerman go on a journey to find the father they have never known but return home with the realization that they may never know him.

The Wednesday Wars. By Gary D. Schmidt. 2007. HMH, $16.99 (9780618724833).
> Seventh-grader Holling Hoodhood has a tough time at school, but at home he struggles to please his father, who puts his work as an architect above his family.

What Daddy Did. By Neal Shusterman. 1991. Harper, $4.99 (9780780719996).
> Preston Scott's father is coming home after being in prison for killing his wife. Based on true events, the story raises interesting questions about the power of love.

What I Heard. **By Mark Geller. 1987. Harper, o.p.**
> When 12-year-old Michael takes a telephone call intended for his father, he becomes disturbed and begins to examine the true meaning of love and forgiveness.

Wolf Rider: A Tale of Terror. **By Avi. 1988. Simon Pulse, $7.99 (9781416954446).**
> A father and son's relationship is threatened when a series of terrifying events raises questions between them.

CLASS DISCUSSION

After the class has read *Somewhere in the Darkness*, engage students in a discussion that encourages inquiry and close reading of the text by utilizing the following questions:

- There are many kinds of families. What words would you use to describe a family? Describe Jimmy's relationship to Mama Jean. Discuss the things that make them a family.
- What evidence is there that the people who live around Jimmy feel "a sense of neighborhood"?
- At what point in the story does Jimmy realize that Crab has broken out of jail? Jimmy appears afraid of Crab. When does Jimmy cease being afraid of his father?
- Several times Jimmy considers returning to New York. Why doesn't he?
- What scenes in the novel reveal that Jimmy is a sensitive person?
- Why do you think Jimmy finally shows Crab the $50 that Mama Jean has given him? Why doesn't Crab take the money when Jimmy offers it?
- "Crab could be so many different ways it was hard to figure him out. He was one way with Mama Jean, another way with Mavis, and another way with Frank." Describe how Crab acts with each of these people. How are his actions akin to his relationship with each of these people?
- Explain the statement "We don't want to bust into Arkansas looking like panhandlers."
- What does Crab mean when he says, "A man finds peace in his sons, and a woman finds life in her daughters"?

- Why does Jimmy say that he will never return to Marion, Arkansas?
- What are Crab's "prison dreams"?
- Jimmy says, "Crab had found something tougher than he was." What do you think is Crab's toughest moment?
- What is the significance of the title of the book?

IN THE CLASSROOM

- Jimmy's teacher is concerned about his skipping school and says to Mama Jean, "The boy has got to realize how important education is." Research the lives of Mary McLeod Bethune and George Washington Carver. Write a paper discussing their contributions to education for African Americans.
- "He [Jimmy] was way behind, but he knew that none of the other kids didn't have any more going for them. Only they didn't have a bad attendance record." Inquire about programs in your school district and community that provide help for students who, like Jimmy, have attendance problems. Role-play a scene in which you try to convince Jimmy to participate in one of these programs.
- Write diary entries that Jimmy might have written for every day of his trip.
- Have students choose one of the other books dealing with strained father-son relationships. Instruct them to write a paper comparing Crab and Jimmy's relationship to that of the father and son in the novel selected.
- Write a biographical sketch that tells about Jimmy 10 years from now.

January 2016

GOTCHA DAY

hen I was 7 years old, I visited an orphanage in Ohio, where my aunt was a social worker. I have a vivid image of the cottages where the kids lived, the playground with swings and slides, a merry-go-round, and rows of bicycles and tricycles of all sizes. I was in awe of the playrooms with dolls, tea sets, trains, trucks, and games. I thought these kids must surely be rich. It didn't dawn on me that they didn't have parents to go home to at night, or that the play equipment was donated by someone who needed a charitable write-off. Instead, it seemed like a summer camp or a boarding school like the Catholic one that Madeline, the heroine of Ludwig Bemelmans' books, attended: their beds were perfectly aligned in one big room. By the time the tour was over, I sensed that these kids weren't like Madeline and that they were living in cottages on this campus for reasons that no one bothered to explain.

People didn't talk about unwanted children in those days. I had not yet met Anne Shirley in Lucy Maud Montgomery's *Anne of Green Gables;* Frances Hodgson

Burnett's Sara Crew, the main character in *The Little Princess;* or Mary Lennox, the protagonist in Burnett's *The Secret Garden.* I was far too young to know Oliver Twist. When I returned home, I went to the public library and borrowed *The Boxcar Children,* by Gertrude Warner. What was it about Henry, Jessie, Violet, and Benny Aden that captivated me? I don't remember focusing on the fact that they didn't have parents. I just thought it was nifty living in a boxcar. At least they were together. The kids I met at the orphanage lived in groups according to their age, not with their siblings, if they had any.

I knew nothing about the historical orphan trains, and I didn't know a single person who lived in foster care. I did eventually know a few adopted children, but the trend in those days was to keep adoptions a secret until it was thought that the children were old enough to deal with the truth. I knew some adolescents who suffered severe emotional issues when they learned of their adoption. Later, when I was teaching children's literature, we read *The Great Gilly Hopkins,* by Katherine Paterson; *Toby Lived Here,* by Hilma Wolitzer; *Missing May,* by Cynthia Rylant; *Baby,* by Patricia MacLachlan; and *Gib Rides Home,* by Zilpha Keatley Snyder. A student in my class shared that she was adopted and that she was the focus of two yearly family celebrations—her birthday and her Gotcha Day (the day her parents adopted her). I thought this was a great idea. I called my aunt, who by this time had adopted an 18-year-old girl who had lived at the orphanage since age 6. Mary's mother was syphilitic and couldn't care for her, but Mary couldn't be adopted until she was emancipated. As a high school graduation gift, my aunt and uncle adopted Mary, and my entire family embraced her. Her diploma became the path to her adoption papers.

This is what I learned from the time I visited that orphanage at age 7 and the time Mary entered our lives. All kids, regardless of age or their living situation, do want parents and do want to belong to a family. This is evident in the Lucky trilogy by Susan Patrone; *Saffy's Angel,* by Hilary McKay; *Heaven,* by Angela Johnson; *Everything on a Waffle* and *One Year in Coal Harbor,* by Polly Horvath; *All the Way Home* and *Pictures of Hollis Woods,* by Patricia Reilly Giff; *Bud, Not Buddy,* by Christopher Paul Curtis; *Three Times Lucky,* by Sheila Turnage; and *Home, and Other Big, Fat Lies* and *What I Call Life,* by Jill Wolfson.

My aunt and uncle sent Mary to college, but after one semester, she asked to come home. A psychologist encouraged them to bring her home and allow her to commute to a nearby university. She had already lived in an institutional setting. She finally had a family and didn't want to leave them. My aunt said that there were Saturday and Sunday mornings when Mary would come and stretch out across the foot of their bed. There, they talked over any issues she might be experiencing. She had missed that part of her childhood, too. Everyone needs that closeness, and, thankfully, my aunt and uncle allowed her to do that.

What happened to Mary? She became a teacher and gave my aunt and uncle three handsome grandsons. She died of a cerebral hemorrhage just a few years after my aunt died, at age 90. Until the day Mary died, I sent her a card on her Gotcha Day. She did indeed belong to our family.

January 2013

TALKING WITH
RITA WILLIAMS-GARCIA

et in 1968, Rita Williams-Garcia's _One Crazy Summer_ (2010) takes three sisters from Brooklyn, where they live with their father and grandmother, to Oakland, California, to meet Cecile, the mother they don't remember. While in California, the Gaither sisters are thrust into the social movements of the 1960s, and by the time they return home, they have even won a small piece of their mother's heart. _One Crazy Summer_ was nominated for the 2010 National Book Award for Young People. In 2011, it was named a Newbery Honor Book, a Coretta Scott King Author Award winner, and the Scott O'Dell Historical Fiction Award winner.

The Gaither girls are not the only ones who have changed while visiting Cecile. In _P.S. Be Eleven_ (2013), also a multi-award winner, the girls return home to find their father engaged to Marva Hendrix, and their grandmother, Big Ma, feels a little less needed. Even more unsettling, Uncle Darnell returns from the Vietnam War a broken man and moves in with the Gaithers. Delphine deals with

these changes by writing long letters to Cecile, who advises her oldest daughter to just "be eleven."

In the following conversation, the celebrated author discusses the creation of her indelible characters and the challenges of setting personal stories within a tumultuous period in U.S. history.

SCALES: Your books are character driven. Who or what was your inspiration for Cecile?

WILLIAMS-GARCIA: I loved writing Cecile. She is an amalgam of sorts. My mother, "Miss Essie," is probably the prototype for all strong characters in my stories. She was a force that no one wanted to reckon with—not even doctors and attendees in her final days. She was very creative, expressive, funny, and kind, but she could be volatile. We had a great childhood, but it wasn't always easy. I thought a lot about female artists of the period while writing Cecile—women with children who struggled to incorporate art and motherhood, and also women who chose to be childless. I returned to my favorite poets of the 1960s, such as Nikki Giovanni, Sonia Sanchez, Lucille Clifton, Gwendolyn Brooks, and June Jordan, and I looked at the lives of the women in the Black Panther movement. I knew I would never have

Cecile apologize, even at the risk of having her misunderstood or not liked by readers. There are reasons why she cannot be with her children, and I respect them all.

SCALES: Some writers say that they connect with young readers because they have total recall of their childhood. What part of your childhood is woven into the Gaither girls' story?

WILLIAMS-GARCIA: I grew up in the same time period and remember so much, but it's my relationship with my siblings that I drew from. We were 13 months apart and did everything together. My older brother, Russell, and

I fought all the time, and our older sister, Rosalind, maintained order. We were great planners and were forever setting off on adventures. It was always understood that we were to mind Rosalind, and we did. Mostly.

SCALES: With which character do you most identify?

WILLIAMS-GARCIA: That's tough. Like Delphine, I was a boy fighter and word lover who spun straw whenever an explanation was needed. Like Vonetta, I was both stagestruck and had bouts of stage fright. I was always in my own little world like Fern, but I wasn't as cute.

SCALES: I have a soft spot in my heart for Pa, because he thinks it is important that his girls know their mother. How does he know that this is the right time for them to meet her?

WILLIAMS-GARCIA: Coming out of this era, Pa would have felt there were things that only a mother can teach her daughters. With Delphine growing in every possible way, and her sisters not too far behind her, he might have felt the urgency for the girls to know their mother. I like to think that Pa saw bits of Cecile in his daughters and that they should at least fill the void with the actual person—crazy and all. He knew Delphine would one day explain Cecile to Vonetta and Fern, even if he couldn't. Plus, now that they were no longer babies, and that Delphine could keep her sisters in line, Cecile would be able to tolerate them for a short period. Yes, tolerate. He hoped for the best for mother and daughters—that they would fill in some of those hard-to-fill spaces.

SCALES: What do you hope your readers learn from Delphine?

WILLIAMS-GARCIA: I hope Delphine confirms for my readers how love of family is both basic and complicated, and that this is all right. Some of my readers must learn to insist on their childhoods in spite of their circumstances, while most, I hope, will value and enjoy their childhoods. Thankfully, I had a long childhood. Not everyone can say that, especially Delphine.

SCALES: As much as Big Ma provides a stable home for the Gaither sisters, I really like that they get a stepmother in *P.S. Be Eleven.* How does Marva allow the girls to grow in ways that Big Ma would never allow?

WILLIAMS-GARCIA: Delphine sees college girls packing up their Volkswagen Beetle with a NOW sticker on the bumper—a little heads-up that women's liberation was headed to Herkimer Street. Pa and Big Ma have done the best that they could, but only Marva can challenge traditions of the past. Marva believes women can accomplish anything if they put their minds to it, and although the message is new, it isn't lost on the Gaither sisters. As much as Marva Hendrix challenges tradition, she also challenges Delphine, Vonetta, and Fern to shake things up a bit. It means Delphine must give up some of her control, especially if her sisters are to grow. Thanks to Marva, the Gaither girls will be wearing jeans and Afro puffs before Big Ma can say, "Grand Negro spectacle."

SCALES: You were only 11 years old in 1968 when *One Crazy Summer* is set. What do you remember about that year?

WILLIAMS-GARCIA: What a dynamic year, 1968! I have my diary from 1967 through 1968, and I remember so much, including the clothes that I wore, my friends, the books that I read, my favorite and least favorite homework assignments, my science fair projects, the games we played, and Friday afternoon catechism. I also remember seeing Vietnam on the living-room television and writing letters to my dad. I remember my mother's work with the Anti-Poverty Program and seeing Dr. Martin Luther King marching, also on TV. It was the year my father returned from Vietnam, and we went to hear Senator Kennedy speak at Monterey Airport. I remember King's assassination, then Bobby Kennedy's assassination, and the manhunts following each one. I remember war protestors shouting at my father when he was in uniform and him saying, "That's what I'm fighting for—your right to say what you want to say." I remember "Happening '68," and a parade of pop stars, but I especially remember the first time I heard James Brown on the radio singing, "Say It Loud—I'm Black and I'm Proud."

SCALES: How is your child's-eye view different from what you later read about the era?

WILLIAMS-GARCIA: As a child, my eyes and ears were open. I wanted to know what was going on, whether my parents were whispering about relatives who were involved in the cause, or whether I was watching the Black Panthers on David Susskind's or David Frost's shows. I read Eldridge Cleaver's *Soul on Ice* and Jason Epstein's *The Trial of Bobby Seale* and had thought Angela Davis and George Jackson were part of a Black Panther love story. As a child, I had romanticized ideals of the movement but was afraid of the movement at the same time. As an adult, I think more of how the movement had been broken down and how it ultimately imploded. Although the romanticized parts have been washed away, I still believe the movement was at its best when it was a grassroots organization that looked out for the rights of poor and working-class communities.

SCALES: Do you know how your novels will end when you begin writing?

WILLIAMS-GARCIA: I always know how my novels will end before I start. That's the only way I can begin the journey. Then, somewhere during the journey, the characters overrule me. Or a plot thread doesn't pan out. Or the first draft is too weak to support the ending. Or, more than likely, I learn something I didn't know when I began and have to regroup. Endings are hard, but endings are the litmus test for the promise of the novel. You know when you've struck that resonating chord. You also know when it's a tad flat. And if you don't know, that's when your editor takes you by the hand and asks you to look at the ending again.

SCALES: You have said that you don't like dealing with racial issues in your novels. How do your books transcend race?

WILLIAMS-GARCIA: Race is complex. It isn't as black and white as resolving an issue between black people and white people. I have a disdain for books that treat race in that simplistic way. As with *One Crazy Summer* and *P.S. Be Eleven*, people of color, specifically African Americans, have much to confront in just dealing with our own outlook based on institutionalized racism and personal and familial experience. It is a leviathan that I won't pretend I can wrap up in a book. But I can write from a place of truth inherent within the characters. For example, my young black male protagonists (including Thulani in *Every Time a Rainbow Dies*) know what a patrol car or police officer could mean. Racism is part of the American fabric. It's in the air. Even when my characters are not fully conscious of it, they're still breathing the air.

What readers connect to in the stories is that, at their core, they are human stories, first and foremost. I can include dozens of icons, events, historical figures, and slogans from the period, but it's always that Delphine is doing a hard, thankless job that makes readers root for her. It's that the readers are drawn in by these funny sisters who so badly want a mother but are sorely disappointed and afraid when they meet Cecile. The readers simply care for the characters, identify with their yearnings, and can laugh with and at them. We've all wanted to impress someone and to be loved and know that we are special. We all know how it feels to fail no matter what we do, or to feel strong in a small body. These are all things we know as humans.

SCALES: The pacing and tone of your writing are brilliant. You provide humor in just the right spots. Is it more difficult to write poignant scenes or humorous ones?

WILLIAMS-GARCIA: I think the humorous scenes are harder. Humor requires timing and a knack for what's funny. The humor works when it springs out of characters being themselves in tense situations. But, honestly, I die like a Borscht Belt comic doing *Def Comedy Jam* when I try to write funny. Just die. Poignant scenes . . . those are special. Quiet. They have to ring true and have an air of inevitability with the right amount of surprise or wonder.

SCALES: What has been the response from young readers to *One Crazy Summer* and *P.S. Be Eleven*?

WILLIAMS-GARCIA: I can't begin to tell you how tremendous the reactions from the readers have been. I hear from girls and boys, teachers, librarians, parents, grandparents who remember those times, reluctant readers—you name it! My favorite responses come from those who are sharing this story within their families across generations, and those who pick up the book by accident. The response has been so tremendous that I've written a final story about the Gaither family called *Gone Crazy in Alabama*. It's so hard to say good-bye to characters I know like family!

SCALES: What might Delphine say about all the awards *One Crazy Summer* has received?

WILLIAMS-GARCIA: Delphine might say, "I don't dare tell Vonetta about all those medals. She'll claim all the credit for being 'the crazy one' in *One Crazy Summer*." Big Ma would want to have a word with me for airing the family business in a book for all to read.

SCALES: You have written for almost every age. Which is your favorite age? Or do you let the story dictate the audience?
WILLIAMS-GARCIA: I have a story that's begging me to write it, and that determines the audience. I'm enjoying writing middle-grade fiction. These readers ask the best questions and wear their loves and dislikes openly. The stories matter deeply to them. This is not to say I won't write for teens again. I'll be back one day.

SCALES: How are today's children's books different from the ones that you read as a child?
WILLIAMS-GARCIA: The children's books I read in my childhood had a storybook quality to them. I always knew I was reading a story that was being told to me by someone else, and, truthfully, those stories—by C. S. Lewis, Madeleine L'Engle, Scott O'Dell, and Reba Paef Mirsky—transported me to another place. But today's narratives for children are a lot closer to the heart and sensibilities of a child. The writers get down in the trenches of what a child thinks and how she expresses herself.

SCALES: Is there a particular novel that kids read today that you would have devoured at age 10 or 11?
WILLIAMS-GARCIA: I loved stories and comic books and female protagonists. I would have devoured Adam Rex's *The True Meaning of Smeck Day* like it was a crunchy bowl of cereal. Second-grade Rita would have read Nikki Grimes' *Words with Wings* over and over. How that book would have affirmed my need to drift away—which always infuriated my brother and sister! I usually got my call to daydream during kickball games.

SCALES: What advice do you give writing students about writing for children?
WILLIAMS-GARCIA: Love the characters more than you love the concept. The

concept is there to challenge the writer to break new ground, but the characters should live in the hearts and minds of young readers, long after the
last pages have been read.

SCALES: What are you writing now?

WILLIAMS-GARCIA: I've finished *Gone Crazy in Alabama*, but I still think about
the Gaithers, Trotters, and Charleses every day. It's just so hard to say goodbye. But I have to admit, I've been surrounded by female voices for so long,
a change is in order. I'm writing a kind of easy reader about a boy who loses
his grandfather. It's called *Clayton Byrd Goes Underground*. At this point, I
have to stop calling it an easy reader, although I'm hoping my reluctant
readers will sail through it. If I do it right, this small novel will be the place
where hip-hop meets the blues. Wish me luck!

SAMPLING WILLIAMS-GARCIA

Clayton Byrd Goes Underground. 2017. 176p. Amistad, $16.99
  (9780062215918).

Every Time a Rainbow Dies. 2001. 176p. HarperCollins, e-book, $8.99
  (9780061923111).

Gone Crazy in Alabama. April 2015. 304p. Amistad, $16.99 (9780062215871);
  lib. ed., $17.89 (9780062215888); e-book, $9.99 (9780062215901).

Jumped. 2009. 192p. Amistad, paper, $8.99 (9780060760939); e-book, $6.99
  (9780061975714).

Like Sisters on the Homefront. 1995. 176p. Puffin, paper, $5.99
  (9780140385618).

No Laughter Here. 2003. 144p. Amistad, e-book, $6.99 (9780061975752).

One Crazy Summer. 2010. 224p. Amistad, $15.99 (9780060760885); paper,
  $6.99 (9780060760908); lib. ed., $16.89 (9780060760892); e-book,
  $6.99 (9780061966675).

P.S. Be Eleven. 2013. 288p. Amistad, $16.99 (9780061938627); paper, $6.99
  (9780061938641); lib. ed., $17.89 (9780061938634); e-book, $10.99
  (9780062208507).

FURTHER READING

Rita Williams-Garcia's *One Crazy Summer* (2010) and its sequels celebrate
the societal changes brought about by the turbulent 1960s. *Book Links* has

explored this important decade in recent issues (most recently in the September 2014 issue, which included the bibliography "Freedom Summer Book Connections"). The focus of the following list is on family connections, rather than historical ones. In the books below, the main characters, like the Gaither girls, are in search of a parent they have never really known.

Enrique's Journey: The True Story of a Boy Determined to Reunite with His Mother. By Sonia Nazario. 2013. 288p. Delacorte, $16.99 (9780385743273); paper, $8.99 (9780385743280); lib. ed., $19.99 (9780375991042); e-book, $8.99 (9780307983152).

> This true story of Enrique, a Honduran boy whose mother left when he was very young in search of a better life in the United States, chronicles his many attempts to find his mother. He is seventeen when he and his mother are finally reunited, but the years apart have taken a toll on their relationship.

The Higher Power of Lucky. By Susan Patron. Illus. by Matt Phelan. 2006. 144p. Atheneum/Richard Jackson, $17.99 (9781416901945); paper, $6.99 (9781416975571); e-book, $6.99 (9781416953951).

> After Lucky's mother dies, her father abandons her and calls upon his ex-wife, Brigitte, to come from France to the small desert town of Hard Pan, California, to take care of his daughter. At ten years old, Lucky longs for a real mother, and as her story progresses through two sequels, *Lucky Breaks* (2009) and *Lucky for Good* (2011), she ponders the question: Does her father really hate her?

It Ain't All for Nothin'. By Walter Dean Myers. 2003. 240p. Amistad, paper, $6.99 (9780064473118); e-book, $6.99 (9780061975004).

> Tippy lives with his grandmother in Harlem, but when she becomes ill, he must go and live with his father, a man he barely knows. His dad isn't interested in being a father, and Tippy is placed in a situation where he must decide whether to take the path toward right or wrong.

Journey. By Patricia MacLachlan. 1991. 112p. Yearling, paper, $5.99 (9780440408093).

> Eleven-year-old Journey and his sister, Cat, are abandoned by their mother, and it is up to their grandparents to help them deal with the fact that she may never return. Journey holds out hope, but eventually he accepts what he cannot fix.

The Search for Belle Prater. By Ruth White. 2005. 176p. Square Fish, paper, $6.99 (9781250008138); e-book, $4.98 (9781429934503).

> In this sequel to Newbery Honor Book *Belle Prater's Boy* (1996), Woodrow

Prater has lived with his grandparents in rural Virginia since his mother, Belle Prater, disappeared more than a year ago. On his thirteenth birthday, Woodrow believes that he has received a message from his missing mother, and he sets out to find her.

Somewhere in the Darkness. **By Walter Dean Myers. 1992. 176p. Scholastic, paper, $5.99 (9780545055772).**

Jimmy Little is motherless, and his father has been in prison since he was a baby, but he has a stable home life in Harlem with Mama Jean, his loving and devoted grandmother. Then, when he is 14, his very ill father escapes and sets out to prove his innocence to his son. In this Newbery Honor Book, Jimmy, in a fit of anger, tells his dad, "You don't know anything about being a father."

Sway. **By Amber McRee Turner. 2012. 320p. Hyperion, paper, $6.99 (9781423137849).**

Ten-year-old Cass has been dreaming of the day that her mother would come home, but after four long months, it appears that her mom is nowhere near ready to return. In the meantime, Cass and her dad set off on a trip in an old RV and form a father-daughter bond that includes a little magic called "sway."

True Colors. **By Natalie Kinsey-Warnock. 2012. 256p. Knopf, $15.99 (9780375860997); paper, $6.99 (9780375854538); e-book, $6.99 (9780375897061).**

In 1952 in Vermont, 10-year-old Blue, abandoned as a baby, sets out to find the mother she has never known. Along the way, she also finds out life-changing things about herself.

Zane and the Hurricane: A Story of Katrina. **By Rodman Philbrick. 2014. 192p. Scholastic/Blue Sky, $16.99 (9780545342384); e-book, $16.99 (9780545633475).**

Twelve-year-old Zane Dupree doesn't know much about his father, who died before he was born, but his mother decides that it is time he meets Miss Trissy, his father's grandmother, in New Orleans. Hurricane Katrina hits the city not too long after Zane arrives, and as he struggles to survive among people he barely knows, he hears boyhood stories about his father and finally makes a connection to the Dupree side of his family.

DISCUSSION

- Big Mama thinks that Cecile is selfish. What is the girls' first impression of Cecile in *One Crazy Summer*? How do they view her by the end of the summer?

- What is the main theme of *One Crazy Summer*? At what point in the novel is the theme first apparent? Debate whether the theme changes in *P.S. Be Eleven*. Quote directly from the novels to support claims.
- In *P.S. Be Eleven*, Delphine says that Cecile is their mother, but she isn't a mom. Discuss the difference. What qualities might each girl want in a mom? Discuss whether Marva Hendrix can be the mom the girls are searching for.
- Why does Delphine need her mother's advice more than Vonetta and Fern? Discuss Cecile's advice to Delphine, "P.S. Be Eleven."
- Have students explain the following quote from *P.S. Be Eleven*: "Twelve makes you know better than to wish for things that only eleven would wish hard for."
- All novels have a conflict. What is the conflict in Williams-Garcia's novels? The climax is the turning point in the novel. Identify the climax of each novel.

IN THE CLASSROOM

- Rita Williams-Garcia frequently uses similes to create certain images. For example, in *One Crazy Summer*, she writes, "Vonetta and Fern stamped their feet like holy rollers at a revival meeting." Ask readers to find other examples of simile in the Gaither sisters novels. Then have them write a simile that best describes Delphine's first impression of Miss Marva Hendrix, Pa's fiancée.
- Lead a class discussion about the most humorous scenes in *One Crazy Summer* and *P.S. Be Eleven*. Then divide readers into small groups and ask them to write one of the scenes as a stage comedy. Cast the play, and perform it.
- Instruct readers to jot down everything that they learned about the 1960s from reading *One Crazy Summer* and *P.S. Be Eleven*. Then have them use books in the library or sites on the Internet to conduct further research on one of the topics (e.g., the Black Panthers) and write a one-page entry for an encyclopedia of the 1960s.

LET'S READ
SHORT SHORTS

ary Soto's *Hey 13!* is a collection of 13 short stories that explore the complexities of growing up. "Twin Stars" defines true friendship through Teri and Luz, inseparable best friends known as Glitz Girls de Southeast Fresno. Saul, the main character in "A Simple Plan," cannot bring himself to abandon his dog though his abusive father insists that the dog must go. In "Musical Lives," Joel has been playing the trumpet for nine years, but he realizes that he will never be any good. When he encounters bullies from the basketball team, he makes the decision to never play in the band at any of their games. Searching for the first kiss is the focus of "A Very Short Romance," and learning the true meaning of religion is the theme of "Finding Religion." The teenage mall culture is revealed in "Celebrities," and the daughter of classic hoarders craves personal space in "Whose Bedroom Is This?" Ashlee is gorgeous but self-centered in "It's Not Nice to Stare," and Freddie, the main character in "Two Girls, Best Friends, and a Frog," loses his intuition

~~and doesn't choose the right girlfriend. In "Altar Boys," Little Ray~~ ~~on January 2015~~
on a Sunday escapade and then must face his mother's wrath. Monica, the
main character in "Romancing the Diary," is brooding over a boy and throws
her cherished diary into a creek. Things look up when a cute 15-year-old boy
from the other side of town rescues the book. "Dirty Talk," the final story,
introduces Tiffany Tafolla, who rethinks the power of profanity when she
hears a young niece of her best friend repeat the language she overhears.

SHORT STORY COLLECTIONS

13: Thirteen Stories That Capture the Agony and Ecstasy of Being Thirteen. Ed.
by James Howe. 2003. 288p. Atheneum, $17.99 (9780689828638); paper,
$7.99 (9781416926849).

> Both humorous and poignant, this collection deals with the awkwardness
> of being 13, as told by well-known writers Ann M. Martin, Bruce Coville,
> Todd Strasser, Rachel Vail, Stephen Roos, Ron Koertge, and others.

Baseball Crazy: Ten Short Stories That Cover All the Bases. Ed. by Nancy E.
Mercado. 2008. 192p. Dial, $16.99 (9780803731622); Puffin, paper, $6.99
(9780142413715); e-book, $6.99 (9781440630019).

> Among the writers in this collection are Jerry Spinelli, Joseph Bruchac,
> and Sue Corbett, and they delve into themes that go far beyond sports,
> such as family and peer relationships.

Baseball in April and Other Stories. By Gary Soto. 2000. 128p. Sandpiper,
paper, $6.99 (9780152025670).

> Set in poor areas of California, these 11 stories deal with typical problems
> of young adolescents.

Because of Shoe and Other Dog Stories. Ed. by Ann M. Martin. Illus. by Alek-
sey Ivanov and Olga Ivanov. 2012. 272p. Holt, $15.99 (9780805093148);
Square Fish, paper, $6.99 (9781250027283); e-book, $9.99
(9781429954983).

> The relationship between dogs and their owners is the theme of these
> short stories by Ann M. Martin, Jon J. Muth, Mark Teague, Margarita
> Engle, Thacher Hurd, Valerie Hobbs, Matt de la Peña, Pam Muñoz Ryan,
> and Wendy Orr.

The Chronicles of Harris Burdick: Fourteen Amazing Authors Tell the Tales. By
Chris Van Allsburg and others. Illus. by Chris Van Allsburg. 2011. 208p.
Houghton, $24.99 (9780547548104); e-book, $18.99 (9780547677606).

> Lois Lowry, Stephen King, Sherman Alexie, and Kate DiCamillo are among

the writers of these 14 short stories based on the illustrations of Van Allsburg's *The Mysteries of Harris Burdick* (1984). The stories range from humorous to spine-chilling to touching.

Favorite Stories for Sharing. Ed. by Avi. Illus. by Chris Raschka. 2006. 342p. Houghton, o.p

This collection of 24 stories includes ones by Richard Peck, Natalie Babbitt, Lloyd Alexander, and Katherine Paterson and deals with cultural diversity, animals as heroes, time machines, and superheroes.

Guys Read: Funny Business. Ed. by Jon Scieszka. Illus. by Adam Rex. 2010. 288p. HarperCollins/Walden Pond, $16.99 (9780061963742); paper, $6.99 (9780061963735); e-book, $5.99 (9780062017635).

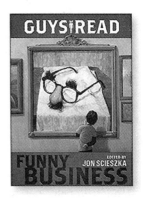

There is humor that is gross and humor that is absurd. Part of the "Guys Read Library," this collection of 10 stories—by writers including Mac Barnett, Adam Rex, David Yoo, Paul Feig, Christopher Paul Curtis, Eoin Colfer, Jack Gantos, Jeff Kinney, David Lubar, and Jon Scieszka—offers both types of humor.

Past Perfect, Present Tense. By Richard Peck. 2006. 192p. Puffin, paper, $6.99 (9780142405376).

This collection of Peck's previously published short fiction and a couple of new ones includes humorous and tragic historical and contemporary stories.

Shelf Life: Stories by the Book. Ed. by Gary Paulsen. 2003. 192p. Simon & Schuster, $17.99 (9780689841804).

The focus of these 10 original stories by well-known authors is how books change lives. Note: sales of this book benefit the organization ProLiteracy Worldwide.

The SOS File. By Betsy Byars and others. Illus. by Arthur Howard. 2004. 80p. Holt, $16.95 (9780805068887).

These 12 first-person stories by students in Mr. Magro's class represent a "fun and extra-credit" assignment where each student writes about a time he or she needed to call for help.

Survivors: True Stories of Children in the Holocaust. By Allan Zullo and Mara Bovsun. 2005. 208p. Scholastic, paper, $4.99 (9780439669962).

In these stories of hope and survival, nine Jewish girls and boys relate true accounts of fear and danger while living in Europe during the Holocaust.

Tales from Outer Suburbia. By Shaun Tan. Illus. by the author. 2009. 96p. Scholastic/Arthur A. Levine, $19.99 (9780545055871).

> These 15 illustrated short stories take readers on a journey from a mundane suburban life to a more magical place filled with wonder, and along the way, they are challenged to pause and think about the important ideas and messages.

Twelve Impossible Things before Breakfast. By Jane Yolen. 1997. 192p. Sandpiper, paper, $6.99 (9780152164447); e-book, $6.99 (9780547996158).

> These scary, gross, and magical stories about a sea monster, fairies, and aliens reveal the breadth of the fantasy genre. The collection also includes modernizations and retellings of old favorites *Peter Pan, Alice in Wonderland,* and "The Three Billy Goats Gruff" (retitled "The Bridge's Complaint").

April 2013

Funny Girl. Edited by Betsy Bird. 2017. 205p. Viking, $16.99 (9780451477316).

> Twenty-eight short stories by bestselling authors like Sophie Blackall and Libba Bray relate just how funny girls can be.

An extensive Readers' Group Guide may be found on the Holiday House website: www.holidayhouse.com/docs/HEY13_Discussion_Guide.pdf.

SIDETRACKED
BY BOOKS

 **find airports almost unbearable. The cacophony of** sounds is enough to give anyone an instant case of attention-deficit disorder. The news screams on television monitors, and airline agents seem determined to outdo CNN by shouting into microphones set to the highest decibel. There are always a few crying babies and a couple of family arguments over starvation versus the high price of airport food. And I do believe that American travelers are in love with their cell phones.

I always travel with a book, and I like to notice what others are reading. To my amazement, many travelers are able to block out the noise and get lost in some sort of reading material. On a recent trip, I looked around and saw a woman reading *Three Cups of Tea* by Greg Mortenson and David Oliver Relin. The young girl sitting beside her was reading the young-readers version of the same book. I decided that they must be a mother and daughter. Across the way, I observed a baby in a stroller gnawing the rounded edges of the board-book version of *Goodnight Moon,* while his mother read aloud Ian Falconer's *Olivia* to his sister. There was a woman reading something on a Kindle, a man reading *World without End* by Ken Follett, and another engrossed in *Run for Your Life* by James Patterson.

It was on this trip that I planned to read Richard Peck's newest book, *A Season of Gifts*. I had just started it when a young man sat down next to me and began playing a game on his iPhone. I glared at him each time his phone signaled a victory, and finally he looked over and said, "I don't like to read. I got sidetracked by sports when I was growing up." He told me that it all began when he was four and his parents enrolled him in T-ball. Then it was Little League baseball, soccer, and basketball. He took golf and tennis lessons in elementary and middle school and swam on the neighborhood swim team in the summer. There was simply no time for reading. When I inquired about the sports he played now, he said, "None, I got burned out." I suggested that he try to become sidetracked with books. He simply laughed and said, "Too late."

I pointed to the baby in the stroller and the baby's sister and said, "Side-tracked." I pointed to the mother and daughter reading the same book and said, "Sidetracked." Then I pointed to the men who were reading and said, "Sidetracked." He went back to his game, and I made a silent vow that I would boycott the first airline that ever allowed cell phones on board.

When I arrived home, I received a call from a young niece who wanted to thank me for the books I sent for her birthday. She told me that she liked reading but that she didn't have much time for reading in school. I cannot believe that a member of my own family has gotten "sidetracked." This time the guilty party is the teacher. My niece, a third-grader, tells me that she has to read for Accelerated Reader, and when she finishes her work, she has to run errands for her teacher. I know exactly what is happening in that classroom. My niece is finishing her work before most of her classmates, and because she has a tendency to become a distraction, the teacher is trying to keep her busy. Why can't the teacher realize that books would take care of the problem?

In spite of what the young man with the iPhone said, it is never too late to grasp the joy of reading. Parents have a lot to do with developing a love of story. Teachers and librarians play a big role too. Allow your students to get "sidetracked" with books, and I just bet that their love of reading will ultimately satisfy at least one of those instructional objectives that we are required to meet. Better yet, create an objective called "sidetracked by books" and just do it.

October 2009

READING
TURQUOISE

**learned to recognize colors long before I started** school. And because I had seen a colorful variety of birds roosting in the trees of our front lawn, I thought I knew something about birds. A few days after school started, my first-grade teacher divided the class into three reading groups: red birds, blue birds, and yellow birds. I was confused. What did birds have to do with reading? Why was one color bird superior or inferior to another? It didn't seem fair to the birds, not to mention to the readers it so blatantly labeled. To this day, I remember heads turning and fingers pointing when kids who could barely recognize Dick, Jane, and Sally's names on the flip chart headed off to their yellow bird group. This label followed these kids to other activities as well. Sometimes no one wanted to sit with them or play with them at recess. Often they were the kids who were kept after school to finish their work or sent to the principal's office for acting out in class. What these kids really needed was a sense of belonging. No one likes to be labeled, especially if the label is negative. I'm not sure when the practice of grouping readers by colors of birds stopped, but I'm quite certain that when it did, "yellow birds" across the nation could be heard chirping their approval.

Such grouping gave way to more individualized reading instruction, but companies like McGraw-Hill, which designed reading curriculums like SRA, couldn't let go of the colors. The result was a box of color-coded cards with paragraphs to read and questions to answer. When each card in the box had been completed successfully, then the reader moved on to the next color.

Perhaps the SRA program worked too well. At a recent ALA conference, a group of colleagues began sharing their "favorite color to read." A good friend of mine, now in her fifties and an avid reader, said that she loved the color turquoise so much that she purposely failed to answer the test questions on the backs of the cards so that she could continue reading turquoise. Her mother was called in for a conference because the teacher couldn't understand the problem. My friend was a good reader. She loved going to the library, and she chose challenging books to read. She even recommended books to her peers. Her mother sat her down and asked her if turquoise was too hard for her. My friend simply answered, "Turquoise is my favorite color. I just like reading turquoise." I'm not sure how they resolved the problem, but being stuck on turquoise didn't leave any lasting scars on my friend. If anything, it provided a lot of laughs over a couple of glasses of wine with a group of librarians who know a thing or two about reading.

Having students read color-coded cards in the classroom wasn't so bad when they were allowed to choose any book in the library they wanted to read. Unfortunately, that's not what kids face now. They are so branded by their reading level that many students complain there just isn't much fun in reading. All kinds of companies have assigned reading levels to children's books that go on library shelves, but so far I don't believe they have color-coded them. Unfortunately, I have heard that some librarians are correlating colors with Accelerated Reader and Lexile reading levels and marking the spines of books. This must be so confusing to kids—not to mention that

there aren't enough colors in the color wheel to match the varied number of reading levels.

What color would you assign to *When You Reach Me,* by Rebecca Stead? How would you color-code *Mockingbird,* by Kathryn Erskine, or *Turtle in Paradise,* by Jennifer L. Holm? What color would you give *The Giver,* by Lois Lowry, when the society in which Jonas lives is indeed colorless? Then there is all the fabulous nonfiction for young readers that many reading programs fail to even recognize. Maybe that's a good thing. Without those reading levels on the spines of the books, students may actually choose to read them.

Given the option, I think that I would rather be "yellow" instead of 4.1, "orange" instead of 5.9, or "blue" instead of 6.2. And I would rather that my reading level remain in the classroom and allow me free use of the library. I'm not sure what reading level corresponds to "turquoise," but what a nice color to wedge into and stay.

— March 2011

AMBASSADOR
OF THE WORLD

**was an adult before I got an official passport, but I** was a child when I first visited another country. The trip didn't require boarding a plane or a ship, but it did require a ticket. It was in the form of a library card. I remember that first trip abroad so well. I stood beside my dad's chair as he read aloud, "In an old house in Paris that was covered with vines, lived twelve little girls in two straight lines." *Madeline,* by Ludwig Bemelmans, was my first introduction to Paris. I fell in love with the City of Light long before I had the chance to stroll the Champs-Elysées or the banks of the Seine. When I did finally get to Paris, the bridges connecting the right and left banks of the Seine were all there, just as Bemelmans painted them. Much later, when I could read on my own, I explored the Swiss Alps, where I met Johanna Spyri's Heidi, Heidi's grandfather, and her best friend, Peter, a goatherd. Then it was on to Prince Edward Island with *Anne of Green Gables,* by Lucy Maud Montgomery.

At the time, I didn't realize how much reading about other cultures shaped one's view of the world or desire to travel to other countries. I simply enjoyed the stories. Then I took a trip through the Andes in Peru and saw llama herders from the window of the train. I said out loud, *"Secret of*

the Andes," a book by Ann Nolan Clark I read in my first children's-literature class; my travel companion didn't understand.

The next year, I was in Spain and felt I had to attend a bullfight to honor Manolo, the main character in Maia Wojciechowska's *Shadow of a Bull.* I sat with my eyes closed for most of the event, but observing the protocol of those in the arena was a cultural experience I will never forget. I understood why Manolo's decision was so difficult. But it was a search for Velázquez's art, which I read about in *I, Juan de Pareja,* by Elizabeth Borton de Treviño, that took me to Spain in the first place. I knew that a number of his paintings were in the Prado, in Madrid, and there, in gallery after gallery, were the

works of Velázquez as well as paintings by El Greco and Goya. I was in heaven until a crowd of American tourists rushed through the galleries in a half hour so that they might go home and say that they had visited Spain's national museum. They didn't see the art at all. But I bet they bought postcards.

I'm sad to say that I encountered the same type of hurried tourists in Amsterdam while visiting the Anne Frank House. Some of these tourists were holding the hands of children who had no idea what the attic rooms represented. I wondered if the tourists had ever read *The Diary of Anne Frank,* and I also had to wonder whether they had exposed their children to books like *A Picture Book of Anne Frank,* by David A. Adler and illustrated by Karen Ritz.

I have been in Third World countries where my knowledge of the culture was limited to the tourist information offered in travel books. And I've even traveled in places in the United States, such as Queens, New York, and border towns in the Southwest, where I was as much a foreigner as I might be in any other place in the world. But there are now so many children's books about other cultures that there is simply no excuse for the young to grow up with a narrow view of the world. Children may someday have the opportunity to cross the Forth Bridge in Edinburgh, kiss the Blarney Stone in Ireland, walk on the Great Wall of China, visit a Buddhist temple in South Korea, or hike to the summit of Mount Kilimanjaro in Tanzania. If so, they should know what to expect before making the journey. They should know because their first "passport," a library card, led the way.

What's on my "bucket list" of places to visit? I would like to go to Vietnam after reading Cynthia Kadohata's *A Million Shades of Gray;* India, because Gloria Whelan made it so enticing in *Small Acts of Amazing Courage;* Hungary, because I loved *The Lace Dowry,* by Andrea Cheng; Ireland, because Patricia Reilly Giff made me fall in love with her ancestors in *Nory Ryan's Song;* and China, because I loved meeting the young Jean Fritz in *Homesick: My Own Story.*

Miss Kanagawa, the Japanese doll that is sent to the United States in Kirby Larson's *The Friendship Doll,* says, "I am above all an ambassador, a dignitary. I simply happen to be a doll." May we always travel with the attitude of an ambassador wherever our passports take us, in real life or through books.

——————————————————————————————— *March 2012*

PART 2

WHAT HISTORY TELLS US

"It wasn't the 'fighting' part of World II that intrigued me. It was the mystery behind the blacked-out words in my uncle's letters and the 'real' families like the Franks who struggled to survive."

MOVING DAY

here is a first-grade reader on my bookshelf that features Dick, Jane, Sally, Puff, and Spot. Mother is shown, usually with a broom or an iron in her hand, while Father is pictured in his workshop using a toolbox. I have a vivid memory of learning to read with these characters. I also remember that I questioned why it was always Mother who put hems in dresses, and Father who fixed wheels on wagons and skates. My mother was good at hems, but she could also build almost anything, which added to my confusion about women's roles.

Once I mastered these stories, I moved on to the more challenging "Alice and Jerry" series. In a story called "Moving Day," Jerry is allowed to ride in the cab of the moving van because he is a boy, while Alice has to ride in the car with her parents because she is a girl. This seemed terribly unfair to me. I thought that Alice had a right to ride in that van too. In those days, teachers focused only on teaching students to read, and they never thought twice about the messages in the books and materials they were using.

As we celebrate Women's History Month in March, I can't help but conjure up memories of those early readers that didn't think too much of girls and women. Today, we can celebrate the fact that girls can not only ride in that moving van, they can drive it too. But sometimes I worry that we have done such a good job of training girls for careers as doctors, scientists, lawyers, politicians, construction workers, plumbers, and electricians, that they take these opportunities for granted, and do little to advance the cause for women. Do they even realize that many of their female ancestors couldn't vote until the Nineteenth Amendment was ratified in 1920? I hope young women remember this when they turn 18. I wonder if they know that there is a Women's History Museum in Seneca Falls, New York. I imagine that few realize the significance of this site for the museum. Do they know about the professional women's baseball teams that played during World War II? Can they possibly pinpoint the time in our society when it became acceptable for women to work outside the home?

Many young women have seen pictures of Rosie the Riveter, but they don't understand what she symbolized. Elizabeth Cady Stanton and Susan B. Anthony have finally made it into history textbooks, but most of the blue jean–clad children and adolescents of today don't realize that they have Amelia Bloomer to thank for such advancement in women's fashion.

I'd like to tell my friends Alice, Jane, and Sally (wherever you are) that women like Alice Paul, Jane Addams, Amelia Earhart, Eleanor Roosevelt, Frances Perkins, Hattie Wyatt Caraway, Rosa Parks, Rachel Carson, Barbara Jordan, and Shirley Chisholm paved the way for girls to do things like ride in the cab of a moving van by their brother's side. And I want them to know that Mother might actually do more than bake cookies and hem dresses. She might work a crane, drive a bulldozer, try a case before the U.S. Supreme Court, or even run for president.

Women's History Month is a good time to raise awareness about the contributions of women to our society. Let us never forget the efforts of those women who led the way. And let us give young girls the leadership skills they need to continue to move forward in the names of Alice, Jane, and Sally, those fictitious characters who never had a chance to realize their potential. Today there are plenty of children's books to guide them.

— March 2008

Amelia Lost: The Life and Disappearance of Amelia Earhart. By Candace Fleming. 2011. 128p. Random/Schwartz & Wade, $21.99 (9780375945984).

The dual narratives relate Earhart's life and her disappearance while revealing the history behind the hype surrounding her unexplained vanishing.

Ballots for Belva: The True Story of a Woman's Race for the Presidency. By Sudipta Bardhan-Quallen. Illus. by Courtney A. Martin. 2008. 32p. Abrams, $16.95 (9780810971103).

Belva Lockwood didn't have the right to vote, but she was the first woman to try a case before the Supreme Court, and she actually garnered votes when she campaigned for the presidency in 1884.

HOW DO WE SAY
THANK YOU,
JEAN FRITZ?

 **have two shelves of books in my office by Jean Fritz.** I wish these were books from my childhood, because I was drawn to biography as a young reader. But I grew up in the 1950s, when the popular biographies for children were from the Childhood of Famous Americans series. By the end of third grade, I had read every title in the series that my library owned. These biographies were highly fictionalized and written to formula, but for some reason they captivated me. I read about Jane Addams and Hull House, Clara Barton and the Red Cross, Florence Nightingale and the field of nursing. Then there was Betsy Ross, who sewed all those stars on the American flag. There was no book about Elizabeth Cady Stanton, and as a result, I knew nothing about the woman's suffrage movement. I think I was in college before I learned that Jane Addams was the first American woman to receive the Nobel Peace Prize.

Then along came Jean Fritz, and everything in the genre of biography for children changed. Known for her impeccable research, Fritz writes about subjects she really admires, and she unveils them with such wit. One young reader once told me, "She makes history so much fun." That she does!

Turn an American historical figure over to Jean Fritz, and sparks go off with such glare that there's a celebration worthy of a Fourth of July parade. She is especially fond of the American Revolutionary War period and has written a number of books about the men responsible for the birth of this

nation: *What's the Big Idea, Ben Franklin?; The Great Little Madison; Where Was Patrick Henry on the 29th of May?; Why Don't You Get a Horse, Sam Adams?; Will You Sign Here, John Hancock?;* and *Shh! We're Writing the Constitution.* Yet there was a slight axe to grind with those men. When they wrote the Constitution, they gave plenty of rights to themselves but few to women. Fritz dealt with the battle that took another century and a half to win when she wrote *You Want Women to Vote, Lizzie Stanton?*

In a biography on one of her publisher's websites, Fritz says that she doesn't find her ideas. They find her. "A character in history will suddenly step right out of the past and demand a book. Generally people don't bother to speak to me unless there's a good chance that I'll take them on." That's exactly what Pocahontas did, and Fritz wrote *The Double Life of Pocahontas.* When Harriet Beecher Stowe got her attention, she wrote *Harriet Beecher Stowe and the Beecher Preachers.* Sam Houston demanded a story, and she wrote *Make Way for Sam Houston.* Teddy Roosevelt bullied his way right into her life, and she penned *Bully for You, Teddy Roosevelt!*

In 1982, Fritz wrote an entirely different kind of book. This time she turned to her own childhood. Born in 1915 to American missionaries in Hankow, China, Jean often felt like an outsider and was homesick for the America she knew only through letters she received from her grandmother. Jean's family returned to the United States when she was 13, but for all of her longing to be a "real American," she found that she was an outsider here as well. *Homesick: My Own Story* was named a Newbery Honor Book in 1983. Perhaps

it was Fritz's desire to be a "true blue American" that made her care so deeply for our country's past. Fritz later returned to China with her husband, Michael, and wrote *China Homecoming,* a poignant account of that visit.

At the age of 95, Jean Fritz published *Alexander Hamilton: The Outsider,* her forty-fifth book, on January 6, 2011. From a girl in China who once felt like an outsider, Jean Fritz has become a true insider in the world of children's books. In 1986, she was awarded the Laura Ingalls Wilder Award by the Association for Library Service to Children for her substantial and lasting contribution to literature for children. And in 1976, she delivered the prestigious May Hill Arbuthnot Lecture. The title of Fritz's lecture, "The Education of an American," was fitting then, and it is fitting now. She has been the ultimate history teacher to generations of young readers. How do we say thank you, Jean Fritz?

January 2011

Jean Fritz died on May 17, 2017, at the age of 101. This is a link to her obituary: https://www.nytimes.com/2017/05/17/books/jean-fritz-dead-childrens-book-author.html?_r=0.

JEAN FRITZ'S
YOU WANT WOMEN TO VOTE, LIZZIE STANTON?

**ife wasn't fair. At least that's what Elizabeth Cady felt** growing up in the early 1800s in Johnstown, New York. The daughter of a lawyer, Elizabeth, known as Lizzie to friends and family, often visited her father's law office, where she witnessed unfair treatment of women. She couldn't understand why the law viewed women as "extensions of their husbands." Why was it difficult for women to own property? Why shouldn't women be allowed to vote? Couldn't women do something beyond rearing children? Why didn't women have the right to the wages they earned? These questions created a fire within young Lizzie, and she began to seek the company of people who shared her feelings. She adored visiting her cousin Libby Smith because Libby's father, Gerrit Smith, was an abolitionist who "didn't talk about obeying laws; he talked about justice." This kind of talk appealed to Lizzie, and her mind began expanding with ideas for changing "the general conditions of women who had no say in anything."

Lizzie's father didn't approve of her visits to the Smith home, and he voiced loud disapproval when she began courting Henry Stanton, an abolitionist and friend of the Smiths. In Judge Cady's eyes, "Henry Stanton was unsuitable in every way." He was 10 years older than Lizzie, had no steady income, spent most of his time speaking for the anti-slavery movement, and his political aspirations left no guarantee for a solid future. Lizzie and her father had long arguments about Henry, and when it became obvious that Judge Cady wouldn't accept Henry, Lizzie decided to elope. Elizabeth Cady and Henry Stanton were married on May 1, 1840. From the beginning, their relationship was different from most marriages in the 1800s. Elizabeth refused to have the word "obey" in her wedding vows, and she never allowed anyone to address her as Mrs. Henry Stanton. On her wedding day, she simply became Elizabeth Cady Stanton.

Immediately following their wedding, the couple set sail for London, where they attended the World AntiSlavery Convention. While there, Lizzie met Lucretia Mott, a Quaker who believed that women should be treated as equal to men. Lizzie was intrigued by Mott, and the two women spent hours talking and exchanging ideas. "She [Mott] put into words all the half-thought-out opinions, all the feelings that Elizabeth had been keeping to herself for years." So, it was on her honeymoon that Elizabeth Cady Stanton pledged her life to woman's rights. Lizzie began speaking her mind, and Henry began to wish that his wife were more "demure." But Lizzie was not to be stopped. She went about voicing her opinions and rearing her family in what was considered a most unconventional way. Henry dealt with the situation by staying away and engaging in his own business of politicking and lecturing. He was not home when any of the seven children were born, although he dropped in now and then to become reacquainted with his family. Lizzie was always glad to see him.

At times Lizzie felt tied down to children and home, and her feelings of frustration escalated when she met Susan B. Anthony. Susan, who had no family, had plenty of time to devote to the woman's rights cause. She urged Lizzie to give up some of her domestic duties and become more active. Lizzie had already spoken at the woman's rights convention in Seneca Falls, New York, in July 1848. Now, there was more work to be done. Susan prodded

Lizzie to use her writing ability and her speaking talents to further represent women. At this point, Lizzie became more active in the battle that had been raging inside her since childhood. She began traveling the nation, speaking her mind and challenging opposing views regarding all issues related to equal rights for women. She wanted divorce laws changed in favor of women, she insisted that women be given the right to own property, and she wanted equal education for women. Above all, she felt that women should be given the right to vote.

Elizabeth Cady Stanton didn't live to see the passage of the Nineteenth Amendment—she died in 1902 at the age of 87. She was remarkable in every way and championed the rights of women until her death.

DISCUSSION

- What is the first hint that Lizzie was a rebellious young girl? Describe her father's feelings toward her.
- Lizzie loved visiting the Gerrit Smith house. How was the Smith house different from the Stanton home? How did these visits shape Lizzie's attitude toward woman's rights?
- Compare and contrast the ideas of the abolitionists with the beliefs of the suffragettes.
- Lizzie liked to think of herself as "selfasserting and defiant." Cite evidence that she lived up to this description from girlhood through adulthood.
- Judge Stanton didn't approve of Lizzie's radical beliefs. Yet, she would never criticize him in print. Why do you think Lizzie chose to spare him her criticism?
- Describe the Stantons' marriage. How did her "mental hunger" and her need for independence influence the way she reared her children?

- Lucy Stone, Susan B. Anthony, and Lizzie were contemporaries who were fighting for woman's rights. How did Lucy's ideas differ from those of Susan and Lizzie?
- Lizzie and Susan became close friends. Yet, Susan always addressed Lizzie as "Mrs. Stanton." Why do you think she never called Lizzie by her first name? How does this contradict their relationship and the ideas of the woman's rights movement?
- What role did men play in the woman suffrage movement?
- Lizzie didn't live to see women gain the right to vote, but she did witness radical changes in society regarding women. What were some of these major changes? Why was it important for these changes to occur before women could gain the right to vote?
- In 1892 Lizzie made her last major speech. It was called "The Solitude of Self" and was considered one of her best speeches. Some students might want to locate and read the speech and tell classmates about it. How did this speech reflect all that she had been fighting for? Why do you think Susan didn't like the speech?

ACTIVITIES

- Design a poster that Lizzie might have carried at the first woman's rights convention.
- Prepare and deliver a speech that Lizzie might have given that outlines the "Declaration of Woman's Rights."
- Lizzie was a good writer, and she often replied in writing to the criticisms that she received from men. Write a reply that she might have written in response to the comment that a "woman is nobody."
- Write a diary entry that Susan B. Anthony might have written on the day of Lizzie's death.
- Construct a pictorial timeline of women's dress, beginning with the bloomers that Amelia Bloomer featured in her magazine and ending with women's fashions today.
- Construct a graph that illustrates the ratio of women and men currently serving in the U.S. Senate and House of Representatives.

RESEARCH

- Lizzie wanted to attend Union College, but the college didn't admit women. Later, Harriot Stanton, Lizzie's daughter, attended Vassar College, one of the schools known as the Seven Sisters. Research the Seven Sisters schools: Vassar, Wellesley, Radcliffe, Mount Holyoke, Smith, Bryn Mawr, and Barnard. Find out when each was founded, what courses each offers, each school's general admissions requirements, and each one's basic philosophy regarding the education of young women. What is the enrollment of each school today? Do these schools now admit males?

- Research the contributions of Betty Freidan and Gloria Steinem to the women's liberation movement of the 1970s. Compare and contrast their efforts with those of Lizzie and Susan B. Anthony.

- Women finally gained the right to vote in 1920 with the passage of the Nineteenth Amendment. At that time, the flappers, called a New Generation of Women, allowed women new freedoms. How did the flappers change life for women in the 1920s?

- Warren G. Harding was elected president when women were first allowed to vote. Research his platform and campaign slogan. What were his views toward women voters?

- Research the purpose of each of the following women's organizations: Zonta International, Actrusa Clubs, American Association of University Women, YWCA, Business and Professional Women, General Federation of Women's Clubs, and the National Organization for Women. Find out if there are local chapters of these organizations in your town or city and how they contribute to the community.

- Using newspapers and magazines, read about the controversy regarding the admission of females to the Citadel, a military college in South Carolina. Write an editorial expressing your views about the issue.

FICTION AND PICTURE BOOKS

Blos, Joan W. *Brooklyn Doesn't Rhyme.* 1994. 96p. Simon & Schuster, $12.95 (0684196948).

> Sixth-grader Rasey Sachs, a first-generation American, writes a composition about the life of her Polish family in the early 1900s, including her mother's involvement in the woman suffrage movement.

Blumberg, Rhoda. *Bloomers!* Illus. by Mary Morgan. 1993. 32p. Atheneum, $14.95 (0027116840); Aladdin, paper, $5.95 (0689804555).

> In this picture book set in the 1850s, Amelia Bloomer, Elizabeth Cady Stanton, and Susan B. Anthony become rebel voices when they don bloomers and begin their crusade for woman's rights.

Duffy, James. *Radical Red.* 1993. 144p. Atheneum, $13.95 (068419533X).

> Twelve-year-old Connor O'Shea and her mother become involved in the woman suffrage movement when they meet Susan B. Anthony in Albany, New York, in 1894.

Lasky, Kathryn. *She's Wearing a Dead Bird on Her Head!* Illus. by David Catrow. 1995. 40p. Hyperion, $14.95 (0786800658).

> Lasky and Catrow amusingly tell the story of how, in 1896, Minna Hall and Harriet Hemenway, founders of the Massachusetts Audubon Society, began encouraging women to join their passionate crusade to preserve bird life.

Levitin, Sonia. *Smile like a Plastic Daisy.* 1984. 192p. Atheneum, o.p.

> Claudia, a high school senior concerned with woman's rights, takes off her shirt at a swim meet to prove a point to the boys and becomes the subject of community debate.

McCully, Emily Arnold. *Ballot Box Battle.* 1996. 32p. Random, $17 (0679879382).

> Young Cordelia is an eyewitness to Lizzie Stanton's attempt to vote in this colorful picture book set in 1880.

Oneal, Zibby. *A Long Way to Go: A Story of Women's Right to Vote.* Illus. by Michael Dooling. 1990. 64p. Viking, $11.95 (0670825328); Puffin, paper, $4.99 (0140329501).

> In 1917, eight-year-old Lila learns from her grandmother, who is involved in the woman suffrage movement, that women have an important role in society.

NONFICTION

Archer, Jules. *Breaking Barriers: The Feminist Revolution from Susan B. Anthony to Margaret Sanger to Betty Friedan.* 1991. 208p. Viking, $14.95 (0-670-83104-2); paper, $5.99 (0140379681).

> Historical essays exploring the feminist movements in America and biographies of groundbreaking feminists connect the past and present feminist revolutions.

Brill, Marlene Targ. *Let Women Vote!* 1995. 64p. Millbrook, $15.90 (1562945890).

> A discussion of the early woman suffrage movement, emphasizing the ratification of the Nineteenth Amendment. An afterword presents contemporary issues regarding woman's rights.

Bryant, Jennifer. *Lucretia Mott: A Guiding Light.* 1995. 144p. Eerdmans, $15 (0802851150); paper, $8 (0802850987).

> A biography of the nineteenth-century Quaker leader who dedicated her life to the abolitionist and early feminist movements.

Dash, Joan. *We Shall Not Be Moved: The Women's Factory Strike of 1909.* 1996. 176p. Scholastic, $15.95 (0590484095).

> An account of the harsh working conditions and the courageous fight by young workers called the Shirtwaist Girls to form the Women's Trade Union League in New York's garment industry in the early 1900s.

Forward into Light: The Struggle for Woman's Suffrage. **Edited by Madeleine Meyers.** 1994. 64p. Discovery Enterprises, 31 Laurelwood Dr., Carlisle, MA 01741, paper, $5.95 (1878668250).

> This collection of journals, news clips, historic photos, poems, songs, essays, and political cartoons highlights the woman suffrage movement in the United States from the days of Sojourner Truth to Alice Paul and Carrie Chapman Catt.

Gold, Susan Dudley. *Roberts v. U.S. Jaycees (1984): Women's Rights.* 1995. 96p. Twenty-First Century Books, $15.98 (0805042385).

> An in-depth look at the 1984 Supreme Court case that banned sex discrimination by private clubs.

Her Story: Women Who Changed the World. **Edited by Ruth Ashby and Deborah Gore Ohm.** 1995. 288p. Viking, $19.95 (0670854344).

> Biographical sketches of 120 women, among them Elizabeth Cady Stanton and Susan B. Anthony, who helped change the lives of women in America.

Hodges, Margaret. *Making a Difference: The Story of an American Family.* 1989. 208p. Simon & Schuster, o.p.; Morrow/ Beech Tree, paper, $4.95 (0688117805).

> In the early twentieth century in Cornwall, New York, Mary Beattie Sherwood leads her five children in trying to bring changes for women, specifically in higher education and voting rights.

Ingraham, Claire, and Leonard W. Ingraham. *An Album of Women in American History.* 1972. 88p. Watts, o.p.

> Beginning with a discussion of the first women in America, this book focuses on prominent American women who made a significant contribution to the struggle for woman's rights and equality.

Johnson, Norma. *Remember the Ladies: The First Women's Rights Convention.* 1995. 176p. Scholastic, paper, $3.50 (0590470868).

> Johnson provides a fascinating account of the first women's rights convention, held in 1848 in Seneca Falls, New York.

Keenan, Sheila. *Scholastic Encyclopedia of Women in the United States.* 1996. 208p. Scholastic, $16.95 (0590227920).

> This reference book, which gives brief and authentically illustrated biographies of 217 women known for their significant contributions to their chosen careers or causes, includes Lucretia Mott, Susan B. Anthony, Amelia Bloomer, Elizabeth Cady Stanton, and Harriot Stanton Blatch.

Kraft, Betsy Harvey. *Mother Jones: One Woman's Fight for Labor.* 1995. 112p. Clarion, $16.95 (0395671639).

> The determined struggle of this Irish immigrant to help the common laborer is told through clear text and numerous black-andwhite photos.

Levinson, Nancy Smiler. *The First Women Who Spoke Out.* 1983. 126p. Dillon, o.p.

> This book presents the lives of six women, including Elizabeth Cady Stanton, Lucretia Mott, and Lucy Stone, who were among the first women to speak for woman's rights.

Rappaport, Doreen. *Their Lives in Their Words.* 1990. 336p. HarperCollins, $18 (069004819X); HarperTrophy, paper, $7.95 (0064461270).

> Presented in the first person through letters, journals, speeches, and so on are the struggles of American women from Anne Hutchinson to today's teenagers.

Rubel, David. *The United States in the 20th Century.* 1995. 192p. Scholastic, $16.95 (0590271342).

> This pictorial chronology of twentieth-century America includes women's

rights issues ranging from the passage of the Nineteenth Amendment to the formation of the National Organization for Women and the long but unsuccessful drive to ratify the Equal Rights Amendment.

Smith, Karen Manners. *New Paths to Power: American Women 1890–1920.* 1994. 144p. Oxford, $20 (0195081110).

This historical view of women at home, at work, and in public life, and of the conditions that led to their social rebellion in the early part of the twentieth century, includes black-and-white photos and a chronology.

Stanley, Jerry. *Big Annie of Calumet: A True Story of the Industrial Revolution.* 1996. 112p. Crown, $18 (0517700972).

Stanley relates the story of Annie Clemenc, the wife of a Croatian copper miner in Michigan's Upper Peninsula, who led daily demonstrations in 1913 against the powerful Hecla Mining Company.

Sullivan, George. *The Day the Women Got the Vote: A Photo History of the Women's Rights Movement.* 1994. 96p. Scholastic, paper, $6.95 (0590475606).

Sullivan provides a photographic account of the woman's rights movement beginning with the 1920 election, when women first voted, and presents chronologically the events that have impacted equal rights for women today.

Alice Paul and the Fight for Women's Rights. By Deborah Kops. 2017. 220p. Calkins Creek, $17.95 (9781629793238).

She was not that well known, but this fierce fighter for women's rights took her battle to the streets, which landed her in jail.

July 1996

TALKING WITH
GENNIFER CHOLDENKO

I n turn-of-the-twentieth-century San Francisco, 13-year-old Lizzie Kennedy lives with her physician father and older brother, Billy. Aunt Hortense and Uncle Karl, the owner of a San Francisco newspaper, live next door in a stately mansion with many servants. Both Lizzie and Billy are strong-willed, but Lizzie is a real challenge for Aunt Hortense, who wants her motherless niece to study the proper behavior of a "lady." Much to the dismay of Aunt Hortense, Lizzie is interested in science, and dreams of becoming a doctor like her father.

While her classmates are chattering about various social functions, Lizzie gets caught up in a dark mystery that has cast a cloud over the city. There is a rumor that the plague has hit San Francisco, and people think it began in Chinatown. Lizzie believes the sudden disappearance of Jing, the family's Chinese cook, is somehow connected with the mystery. Then Lizzie discovers Noah, Jing's son, hiding in his father's third-floor room in the Kennedy's house. Noah fears that his father is caught in the quarantine in Chinatown, where he serves as a translator on his day off.

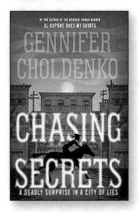

The rumor of the plague heightens, and angry mobs set fire to Chinatown. But Uncle Karl and Dr. Kennedy refuse to acknowledge the ugly truth, and Lizzie and Noah decide it is up to them to piece together the ominous secret that threatens their city and their families.

Rooted in history, *Chasing Secrets: A Deadly Surprise in a City of Lies* offers a strong female character that wants to live life on her own terms. Even Aunt Hortense, who harbors her own secrets, grows to accept Lizzie's dreams. The mystery unfolds with humor and sadness, exposing readers to the social beliefs and day-to-day lives of the people who inhabited San Francisco in 1900. In the following conversation, Choldenko discusses how she approaches research for her historical novels and her writing process.

SCALES: How did you become interested in writing historical fiction?

CHOLDENKO: I love history, so writing historical fiction should have been a no-brainer for me, but it was not. I didn't consider writing historical fiction until I got the idea for the Al Capone books. I was intimidated by the challenge of creating voice in historical fiction. Voice in contemporary fiction requires a finely tuned ear. But no matter how finely tuned your ear may be, you simply don't have the experience of living in a time other than your own. Creating a believable, authentic voice in historical fiction is a daunting challenge.

SCALES: You offer a long list of notes at the end of the novel. Will you take us through your research process?

CHOLDENKO: I've learned to research in the skinned-knee school. I bumble along, I make mistakes, I doubt my sources, I ask questions, I ask more questions, I go to the places I'm writing about, I walk the scenes, and I dig and dig and dig. What seems like a simple question can take a week to answer; a wrong turn can yield a treasure trove of information that may form the backbone of my book. All of this is part of the happy mess called "research."

In the case of *Chasing Secrets,* the research was especially intimidating because so much of the existing nonfiction about the plague outbreak in San

Francisco was contradictory. I could not figure out what actually happened. And then one day I discovered *The Barbary Plague* (2003), by Marilyn Chase. That was the first source I found that I felt confident in. And from that book and its bibliography, I was able to understand what had really happened and why it was so difficult to find the truth.

SCALES: How do you know when the research is done and it is time to write the novel?

CHOLDENKO: My research and writing are interwoven. When the book is printed, I stop researching, but not before. Researching is generally the first step, but until I actually start writing, the research lacks focus. The research gives the writing authority and authenticity. On a good day, I will write in the morning and research in the afternoon.

SCALES: Does the plot take shape in your mind as you are doing research?

CHOLDENKO: Sometimes. More often I write my way into a compelling plot. I pour as much information as I can into my head, and then I begin trying to figure out who my characters are and what drives them. My first plot ideas are generally too generic. But as my characters develop, I then begin to see how their personalities can drive the plot in a fresh direction.

SCALES: What was your inspiration for the character of Lizzie?

CHOLDENKO: There's a little of me in Lizzie, and a little of my daughter, plus a lot of purely made-up stuff. The writing gained real authority from reading memoirs of doctors and of doctor's daughters.

SCALES: I love Aunt Hortense, and Lizzie is such a challenge to her. Which character took shape first?

CHOLDENKO: Lizzie took shape first. Aunt Hortense started out stiff and superficial, but with each draft, she gained depth. In the end, I was surprised how close the bond between Lizzie and Aunt Hortense actually was.

SCALES: How would Lizzie have been a different character if her mother were alive? Did you know from the very beginning that Lizzie would be motherless?

CHOLDENKO: I did not know Lizzie would be motherless. All I knew for sure was Lizzie would have a strong relationship with her father. In my early drafts, Lizzie had a mother. But Aunt Hortense was an important character from the start, and she began to take over in a way I hadn't planned. Soon she was overshadowing Mom, and I began to see that the way to take the relationship between Lizzie and Aunt Hortense to the next level was to make it a more essential part of Lizzie's life. That change helped me bring Lizzie into focus in a deeper way.

SCALES: What questions do young readers ask about *Chasing Secrets*? Are questions from girls different from those of boys?

CHOLDENKO: I haven't noticed a big difference in questions from boys versus girls for any of my books actually. For *Chasing Secrets,* kids want to know how much of the story is true. There are a lot of questions about Billy's character and why I ended the book as I did. I got a letter a few weeks ago from a girl who was incensed that Noah was so sexist.

SCALES: Moose is the male main character in your Al Capone books. How difficult is it to get inside the head of a male character? Will there be another book about Moose?

CHOLDENKO: I am hard at work on the fourth Al Capone book right now. I absolutely love writing from a boy's point of view. It seems to come naturally to me, though I don't really know why.

SCALES: Young readers are intrigued by the titles of your novels. And the subtitle of *Chasing Secrets* suggests a mystery. At what point do you title a novel? Have some titles come to you quicker than others?

CHOLDENKO: I am kind of a fanatic about titles. It is not uncommon for me to come up with 200 title ideas for a novel. Once in a while, a title will come early in the writing process and it will be a perfect fit. That was true of *Al Capone Does My Shirts.* And it was true of the subtitle for *Chasing Secrets.* Other novel titles have required a huge amount of effort. *Notes from a Liar and Her Dog* would come under that category. I had something like 257 title ideas for that book. I've had two novels that have been titled by other people. My editor came up with the title *Chasing Secrets,* and a fan titled *Al Capone Does My Homework.*

SCALES: You have a degree from the Rhode Island School of Design. How is writing different from being a visual artist?

CHOLDENKO: I have a new picture book due out in 2017 called *Dad and the Dinosaur,* illustrated by Dan Santat. The experience I gained in art school was essential to my picture-book writing skills. Also, two of the novels under contract will be illustrated novels. My illustration background has helped me to understand how powerful illustration can be, and how important it is not to keep illustration in a box—literally and figuratively. Words and pictures can play off each other to create a story, which simply would not be possible with words or with pictures alone.

SCALES: *Al Capone Does My Shirts* was named a Newbery Honor Book. How did that change your life as a writer?

CHOLDENKO: I don't think it changed my life as a writer, but it certainly changed my life as a person. Winning that award altered my perception of myself. In my head, I was not the kind of person who stood on center stage, and yet there I was.

SCALES: What are you writing now?

CHOLDENKO: I have four novels under contract right now. I'm working on two at the moment: a revision for a middle-grade novel, which is on the younger side of middle grade, and a revision for the fourth Al Capone book. I would tell you the title of the Al book, but right now my editor doesn't know I've retitled it. If she reads this interview, she's going to be surprised.

SAMPLING CHOLDENKO

Al Capone Does My Homework. 2013. Dial, $17.99 (9780803734722).

Al Capone Does My Shirts. 2004. Putnam, $17.99 (9780399238611).

Al Capone Shines My Shoes. 2009. Dial, $17.99 (9780803734609).

Chasing Secrets: A Deadly Surprise in a City of Lies. 2015. Random, $16.99 (9780385742535).

A Giant Crush. Illus. by Melissa Sweet. 2011. Putnam, $16.99 (9780399243523).

If a Tree Falls at Lunch Period. 2007. HMH, $7.99 (9780152066444).

No Passengers beyond This Point. 2011. Dial, $16.99 (9780803735347).

Notes from a Liar and Her Dog. 2001. Putnam, $6.99 (9780142500682).

Putting the Monkeys to Bed. Illus. by Jack E. Davis. 2015. Putnam, $16.99 (9780399246234).

FURTHER READING

Below, find a list of titles that can be read in conjunction with *Chasing Secrets* to help readers gain a greater sense of America in the early twentieth century, and of San Francisco in particular.

America in the 1900s and 1910s. By Jim Callan. 2005. Facts on File, $35 (9780816056361).

> The social, political, and technological events of the first two decades of the twentieth century are briefly presented, and are supported by sidebars and images, in this entry in the Decades of American History series.

Bubonic Panic: When Plague Invaded America. By Gail Jarrow. 2016. Boyds Mills/Calkins Creek, $18.95 (9781620917381).

> Illustrated with historic photographs, this well-researched and detailed work chronicles the plague that terrorized San Francisco in 1900, and offers a discussion of the risks of plagues today. A timeline, glossary, and index are all included.

Dragonwings. By Laurence Yep. 1975. HarperCollins, $6.99 (9780064400855).

> This 1976 Newbery Honor Book tells the story of eight-year-old Moon Shadow Lee, who crosses the Pacific to join his father in San Francisco's Chinatown in the early twentieth century.

Hattie Ever After. By Kirby Larson. 2013. Delacorte, $8.99 (9780375850905).

> In this novel, set in early twentieth-century San Francisco, Hattie Brooks dreams of becoming a journalist like her hero, Nellie Bly, but to do that, she must tackle big-city life with courage and conviction, and she must settle issues related to matters of the heart.

Women's Right to Vote: America's Suffrage Movement. By Katie Marsico. 2010. Marshall Cavendish, o.p.

> This well-researched book in the Perspectives On series offers various perspectives on the suffrage movement in the United States as suffragists worked to ratify the Nineteenth Amendment.

A free and extensive Educator's Guide on *Chasing Secrets* is available on the Penguin Random House website: www.randomhouse.com/teachers/resource/chasing-secrets-educators-guide-with-ccss-tie-ins/.

September 2016

IT'S NOT MY WAR

**have no memory of World War II, but I have a ration** book in my name. It still has stamps. My father's youngest brother was drafted right out of high school, and after a very short basic training sailed to Europe on the *Queen Mary,* a luxury liner used as a troopship. He fought in the Battle of the Bulge, the bloodiest battle involving American soldiers in World War II. My uncle was lucky. He came home. Now in his eighties, I have rarely heard him talk about the war.

When Ken Burns' documentary *The War* aired on PBS, I watched every episode. At the end, I called my uncle. And, this time he talked. I told him that when I was in fourth grade, a friend and I went into the attic of my grandmother's house and discovered a trunk that held letters he wrote home. My grandmother had saved them all, and she had them organized by date. He had no idea that she had done this. It was many years later that I learned that the blacked-out words in those letters were done by censors. For security, I was told. Much later I read *The Diary of Anne Frank,* and I wondered why we had never studied World War II in my history classes.

It wasn't the "fighting" part of World War II that intrigued me. It was the mystery behind the blacked-out words in my uncle's letters, the "real" families like the Franks who struggled to survive, and the sacrifices of the people on the home front. And these were the parts of the Burns documentary that captivated me. These were not actors but "real" people who were willing to share their memories. One of them taught biology at the college I attended. The entire production was a memoir—intended to preserve the battles and the sacrifices, won and lost, both at home and abroad.

The week after *The War* was shown, I asked my niece, who was born after Vietnam, if she had watched it. She replied, "No, it's not my war." World War II wasn't my war either. But my uncle's letters, the unused stamps in my ration book, and Anne Frank's diary were my connection to a period of which I have no memory.

So where is the connection to World War II for today's children? Maybe some of them have family letters, diaries, and pictures that will someday

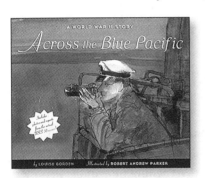

interest them. But they all have novels and picture books. There are those set on the home front like *Across the Blue Pacific: A World War II Story* by Louise Borden, *Coming on Home Soon* by Jacqueline Woodson, *Stepping on the Cracks* by Mary Downing Hahn, *Lily's Crossing* by Patricia Reilly Giff, and *The Art of Keeping Cool* by Janet Taylor Lisle. In addition to *The Diary of Anne Frank,* readers may connect to Jewish families and their struggle to escape the Nazi regime by reading *Number the Stars* by Lois Lowry, *The Upstairs Room* by Johanna Reiss, and *The Night Crossing* by Karen Ackerman. There are books like *House of the Red Fish* and *Under the Blood-Red Sun* by Graham Salisbury and *Weedflower* by Cynthia Kadohata that show the unfair treatment of Japanese Americans who were held in U.S. internment camps after the bombing of Pearl Harbor. Even the gory details of the battles are there in books like *The Last Mission* by Harry Mazer. And what are the lessons to be learned from World War II? These can be found in books and documentaries as well. The preservation of story is the only way to help children make the Second World War their war too.

TALKING WITH
GRAHAM SALISBURY

n December 7, 1941, the Japanese attacked Pearl Harbor, on the Hawaiian island of Oahu. The United States suffered thousands of casualties on board the *USS Arizona*, but Japanese Americans living in Hawaii suffered as well. Many were herded off to internment camps, most endured cultural prejudices, and some lost their jobs.

Graham Salisbury writes about this heart-wrenching time in the Prisoners of the Empire series. *Under the Blood-Red Sun* (1995) is the first book in the series and tells the story of eighth-grader Tomikazu Nakaji, who is playing in a field with his best friend when the Japanese planes attack. Life changes for Tomi when his father and grandfather are taken to an internment camp, his father's fishing boat is sunk, and his grandfather's racing pigeons are killed. Tomi is now the man of the family in *House of the Red Fish* (2006), and he deals with bigotry from many on the island. He sets out to find his father's fishing boat and fix it so that his family may fish again.

Eddy Okubo is the main character in *Eyes of the Emperor* (2007), the third book in the series. After lying about his age and enlisting in the U.S. Army, he runs head-on into bigotry. Zenji Watanabe, the main character in *Hunt for the Bamboo Rat* (2014), enlists in the U.S. Army and is sent to Manila as a Japanese interpreter. Though he is interrogated and tortured by the Japanese, he remains loyal to the United States.

In the following conversation, Salisbury discusses these books, as well as his popular Calvin Coconut series for younger readers. The Japanese surrendered to the United States on September 2, 1945, marking the official end of World War II. Since the seventieth anniversary of this date is approaching, the bibliography accompanying this interview is specifically linked to the Pacific theater.

SCALES: Would you describe your childhood in Hawaii?

SALISBURY: Until seventh grade, I essentially raised myself. I was wild, just out there roaming the neighborhood in Kailua, Hawaii. I had a gang of great friends, a bike, and the most beautiful beach on the island as a playground. I had a copy of [Edgar Rice Burroughs'] *Tarzan of the Apes* and a forbidden military station in the dry jungle over the hill and out of sight from the rest of the world. My life was awesome! I had three younger sisters, who were just as wild as I was, but I didn't think much about them. They were on their own, as far as I was concerned. My friends and I were too busy digging tunnels in the sand, hidden in the trees where no adult could ruin it by telling us that the unsteady sand might cave in and kill us. We were indestructible.

My mom—a single mom at the time—was about to go crazy with worry about how we were growing up. To deal with it, she found a teenager from Texas to come live with us and attend school. Her job was to "watch" over us kids. My life changed when she moved in. I got kicked out of the house into a storage room in the stinky garage. And it was awesome! I had my own apartment!

That was the setting that formed me into the freedom-loving person I am today, only the freedom I had back then was completely untamed. At the time, I could have asked for nothing more. But having no parent, so to speak, left me wanting (very badly) for some kind of foundation. I needed someone to tell me—even better, to show me—how to live a life, saying, this is good; this is not; this is how you do it; this is how you don't do it. I had nothing like that. I had no anchor.

SCALES: On your website, you say you needed "limits," and you found them in boarding school. How did this discovery prepare you for being a writer?

SALISBURY: When seventh grade rolled around, my exasperated mom gave me the greatest gift of my life: she kicked me out of the house. Permanently. She sent me away to boarding school on the Big Island of Hawaii. I never lived at home again. And there, at that prep school (Hawaii Preparatory Academy), I found the trailhead, the starting-off point, the faint beginnings of hope and possibility. There was this gutsy guy, our headmaster. He taught us values. He stretched and broadened our horizons. "You boys do not have to be idiots. Hitch your wagon to a star," he said over and over. "Reach, grow, become the best you can be. You are a miracle. Don't you know this?"

It is around this great lesson that I build my books. There is nothing more important, in my opinion, than to pass along what I have learned to those who follow. I say to readers, especially boys, "You don't have to drift. You can find your star; you can soar. You decide. If you don't, someone else will. Is that what you want?"

SCALES: Which of your characters do you feel most needs "limits"?

SALISBURY: This is something I have never thought about. In looking at my collection of characters, what I see is a bunch of good guys trying to make their way in the world. However, there is one character who fits the intent of this question: Keet Wilson, in *Under the Blood-Red Sun.* This boy is a good kid under his skin. But his foundation is shaky; he has been let down by the people in his life, most notably by his own father, who has successfully taught him how to live a prejudicial life. Keet runs free. No one checks his whereabouts. No one really cares. In this environment, he doesn't have much of a chance. It's Tomi, the hero of the story, who ultimately shows him how to live with integrity. It's a dynamic I am quite familiar with. I can see it so clearly now, looking back.

SCALES: I know that you are from a family of journalists. You say you became a novelist because "you chose to imagine rather than report." How do you blend both imagination and reporting to write historical fiction?

SALISBURY: With historical fiction, I take the facts of my research, like one might pick up brand-new bars of colored clay, and with those facts, I bend, twist, soften, and mold a story with structure, a premise, rising action, successes and failures, and closure. Many times, historical events are recounted more as slices of life than story, so it's the art of the historical novelist to transform facts into emotions that tell the deeper story, the one that lives in the heart. There is hardly anything more rewarding than finding success in doing this. When your own heart cries, you have found truth.

SCALES: How did you approach the research for the WWII novels? How did you know when the research was complete and you were ready to write?

SALISBURY: I begin with reading, which is kind of like hiking in the woods, looking for arrowheads. My first goal is to find a "gem," something unusual or unheard of, something that excites me, something that has me saying, "Oh, oh, oh! This story has to be told!" I need that gem first and foremost, because it will be the thing that makes my heart cry, the thing that will give me the passion to push through one or two years of intense work. My research is done only when my editor sends the manuscript back to me for revisions. I research every little detail. Research is key. It's also fun. But you have to keep it tame. If it's wild, it can become an amazingly effective procrastination tool.

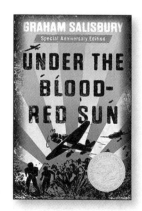

SCALES: What was the most interesting piece of information that you uncovered in your research?

SALISBURY: Pigeons. They appear as the high point in *Under the Blood-Red Sun.* One of my primary sources was a Japanese man who was 11 years old on the day Pearl Harbor was bombed. The day after the bombing, the FBI told him to kill his 35 racing pigeons because there was a possibility that his birds might be used to communicate with the enemy. They also asked him how long his family had been sending messages to the enemy. My first reaction was not that the birds were killed, but rather why had I never heard of such a thing. This is what I call a gem.

In a companion novel, *Eyes of the Emperor,* 25 young Japanese men from Hawaii were used in a war-dog training program in the Gulf of Mississippi, only these guys weren't used as trainers (handlers); they were used as bait. A Swiss hunting guide had sold President Roosevelt on the notion that Japanese people had a particular odor that dogs could be trained to trace.

SCALES: You were born a year after WWII ended. At what age were you first aware of the prejudices against Japanese Americans by the U.S.?

SALISBURY: As a kid, I was clueless. I had no books, no teachers who brought it up. I had no parent who talked with me about this part of our history. There wasn't anyone who warned that if we didn't pay attention to such prejudices, we would make the same mistakes over and over. No one wanted to talk about it, and the Japanese in Hawaii had too much humility to complain, even after the enormous sacrifices they made. I first became aware of the tragedy foisted upon Americans of Japanese ancestry when I was beyond college. Teachers today are far more aware of bringing injustices like this to light, and I hope to help them with my work as a writer. There is great power in awareness. I can't tell you how much respect I have for the young Japanese American men of the WWII generation.

SCALES: How have Japanese Americans in Hawaii received your WWII novels?

SALISBURY: I believe very well. Their history needs to be told, and I don't think they mind having an outsider tell it along with writers of their own. We are all Americans. I have recently been given the great honor of being designated as an Honorary Member of the all-Japanese 100th Battalion Veteran's Club. I value this above all honors I have ever received.

SCALES: Do you think that young readers see a connection between Japanese American profiling in the U.S. after Pearl Harbor and the profiling of Muslim Americans after September 11?

SALISBURY: The independently brilliant ones do, but most will only see that connection if an excellent teacher, parent, or mentor has raised their awareness. Today's young people are bombarded with distraction, and to help them get past it and recognize the connections is a job for the adults in their lives. Books and films contribute as well.

SCALES: How might stories be used to help Americans understand the dangers of racial profiling?
SALISBURY: Readers understand profiling by standing in Tomi's shoes in *Under the Blood-Red Sun.* Nothing sends a message like an emotional moment in a story. One feels deep emotion for Tomi and his family when the FBI, for no good reason, take his grandfather away. You don't have to talk about it. The story gives it to you.

SCALES: *Under the Blood-Red Sun, House of the Red Fish,* **and** *Eyes of the Emperor* **are written in first person. Explain why you chose to write** *Hunt for the Bamboo Rat* **in third person.**
SALISBURY: The first three books in the Prisoners of the Empire series were fictions built around particular events, and, as such, maintained a certain distance between the history and myself. *Hunt for the Bamboo Rat* centered on a specific person, and the distance between Richard Sakakida and myself was very close. I did not feel comfortable closing that gap even further with a first-person viewpoint. Out of respect for this heroic man, I felt I needed to maintain a certain distance. The third-person viewpoint gave me that comfort.

SCALES: With which of your characters do you most identify?
SALISBURY: I most identify with Sonny Mendoza, in *Blue Skin of the Sea.* There is a lot of "me" in that book. He is built upon my basic sensibilities. With that book, I was exploring my own father-son issues as well as telling a story about a place. Writing that book was a wonderful, wonderful experience. It will always be my favorite.

SCALES: Which character do you most admire?
SALISBURY: Mikey Donovan, in *Lord of the Deep,* whose integrity was at issue

as he was faced with a very difficult decision, one of those charged gray-area issues where answers are neither right nor wrong, and could be both. He made his decision, and I have nothing but respect for him for it. I'm not sure I would have had his guts, or his insights. But here's the crazy thing about *Lord of the Deep:* I did not know what Mikey's decision would be until the moment I wrote it. And then I had to have a brilliant seventh-grader read my manuscript and tell me what the heck my book was about.

SCALES: The Calvin Coconut series is so needed for its targeted audience. How did you decide to make a shift from more serious novels and write these books?

SALISBURY: I created Calvin Coconut after an unexpected yet oh-so-endearing personal experience. I'd just finished a large, middle-school event, and as I was being escorted out to my car, my teacher-guide mentioned that she had a friend who taught third grade at the adjacent elementary school, and that this friend loved my books and often talked about *Under the Blood-Red Sun* in her classroom and would I mind dropping in just to say hello to the kids. They'd never met an author, and that sure would be a special experience for them.

I had not been in a third-grade classroom since Kailua Elementary School, in Hawaii. We headed over, and the minute we walked in, the entire room fell dead silent, and all eyes grew big as plates. I spent a glorious half hour in that classroom, and when I walked out, my face hurt from smiling so much. As I drove away, it hit me like a hammer: I had just found my people! I can't explain it, but elementary-school kids touch my heart deeply. I had found my place.

So, I invented Calvin Coconut. He was going to be my ticket to visit that age again. It worked! And my writing life leaped forward on a far more personal level. Sometimes I am down in the trenches with them—with the fatherless, the neglected, the homeless, the ones who just need someone to see them. Now my heart is tested in ways I had not known it could be. I have been moved, shifted. I am now so much more aware of my readers. There's that awareness again. And emotion. My teachers. I could not be more fortunate.

SCALES: How is writing for younger readers different from writing for young adults?

SALISBURY: Writing for the younger guys is way easier, because I more or less draw upon my own crazy young days in Hawaii. I get an idea and run with it, often having only the murkiest idea of where I'm going with a story. But here's the best part: when I'm immersed in a Calvin Coconut project, I get that very same inexplicable happiness I felt in that third-grade classroom. So, in that sense, writing for this age is very different. It's me rolling around in the perfect wonder of those years, still untainted by the crush of life.

On the other hand, writing for my older readers puts me in the zone of "challenge." I am almost always thrilled to set out on a new adventure where I learn something new and important and get to figure out ways to share those discoveries with my readers. This kind of writing is tougher. It's a lot of work, a lot of research and brainstorming, all of which I love to do. There is nothing quite like being immersed in an exciting creative project. For me, the process is actually more rewarding than the product. However, the most rewarding experience by far is when I stand surrounded by a mass of antsy third- or fourth-graders, all wanting to know if I'm real.

SCALES: What is your advice to teachers and librarians who have been charged with turning boys into readers?

SALISBURY: Read aloud to your reluctant readers—a whole book. Get them absorbed in the story, by what happens next. Then read only part of a book, maybe one or two chapters, just enough to capture a bit of interest. Make the book available for them to finish on their own. Ultimately, all it's going to take to turn a reluctant reader into a lifetime reader is one seminal book. That's how it worked for me. If an adult is enthusiastic about reading, that enthusiasm can trickle down and settle in on even the most distracted brain. You won't catch them all, but you may catch a few. All we can do is keep on trying.

SCALES: My guess is that your Calvin Coconut fans grow up to become fans of your young adult books. What has been their response to the WWII novels and *Lord of the Deep*?

SALISBURY: The only verifiable connection between my Calvin Coconut books and my novels for older readers is the connection made at the elementary-school level, particularly with my novel *Under the Blood-Red Sun*. Advanced readers in grades four, five, and six often "graduate" to that book even as their peers continue reading Calvin Coconut books. I get tons of elementary-school mail about *Under the Blood-Red Sun*. I even adapted this book to film, which was produced by an amazing film team out of Hawaii. You can see the result here: www.under-

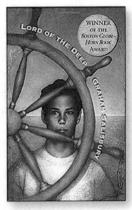

thebloodredsun.com. The continuing success of this book alone has brought the rest of my books to thousands of new readers. It's quite amazing.

SCALES: Take us through a day in the writing life of Graham Salisbury.

SALISBURY: I am a committed worker if I have a solid project going on, but if I am still trying to pull a project together, I am a master procrastinator. Here is how a sample workday goes: I get up at 5:00, and by 6:00, I am at my studio, a 900-square-foot "cabana" on the water, where the very first thing I do is go out on my deck—rain, wind, ice, snow, and all—and thank God and the universe for all the wonder I have in my life. By 6:45, I am at my desk and cranking away. By 10:30, I am ready for a break, so I head to the gym. By 2:00, I am back at it until around 4:00. At that time, I take a meditation break and then arrange my desk for the next day, head home, and take my 16-year-old daughter to dinner. This schedule doesn't always happen that way, but that's what I shoot for.

SCALES: Is it more difficult to write or to teach writing?

SALISBURY: Definitely more difficult to write—you have to make something out of nothing. Teaching is fun. You just talk about what you love to do.

SCALES: What are you writing now?

SALISBURY: Now I'm in fleshing-out-new-project mode, or "research" mode. I have several ideas. I'm waiting for something to jell. What shall I do next? Life is just so dang full of wonder; living is a process; and I'm engaged.

SAMPLING SALISBURY

Blue Skin of the Sea. 1992. 224p. Knopf, $15.95 (9780385305969).

Extra Famous. 2013. 176p. Random/Wendy Lamb, $15.99 (9780385742207).

Eyes of the Emperor. 2007. 256p. Random/Wendy Lamb, $17 (9780756972844).

Hero of Hawaii. 2011. 160p. Random/Wendy Lamb, $12.99 (9780385739627).

House of the Red Fish. 2006. 304p. Random/Wendy Lamb, $16.95 (9780385731213).

Hunt for the Bamboo Rat. 2014. 336p. Random/Wendy Lamb, $16.99 (9780375842665).

Kung Fooey. 2011. 144p. Random/Wendy Lamb, $12.99 (9780385739634).

Lord of the Deep. 2001. 192p. Delacorte, $15.95 (9780385729185). Gr. 6–8.

Night of the Howling Dogs. 2007. 208p. Random/Wendy Lamb, $19.99 (9780385901468).

Trouble Magnet. 2009. 160p. Random/Wendy Lamb, $15.99 (9780385906395).

Under the Blood-Red Sun. 1995. 272p. Random/Wendy Lamb, $17 (9780780753303).

Zippy Fix. 2009. 176p. Random/Wendy Lamb, $15.99 (9780385737029).

A free and extensive Educator's Guide for the Prisoners of the Empire series is available on the Penguin Random House website: www.randomhouse.com/teachers/resource/under-the-blood-red-sun-educators-guide.

April 2015

THEY LAUGHED

**ast year I was invited to speak in Seoul, South Korea.** I was only there a few days, but my hosts wanted me to see the National Library for Children and Young Adults and the National Museum of Korea. It was a Saturday, and the museum was crawling with schoolchildren of all ages. I was told that in Korea children go to school six days a week and that Saturday is often designated a field-trip day. The students were in small groups, and they all seemed to be taking notes. I asked my translator what the children were doing, and she said, "In Korea, we want our children to know our history. They must take notes about what they see." Children taking notes wasn't foreign to me, but the fact that the children traveled in small groups with no chaperones amazed me. I said to my translator, "They are so well behaved." She replied, "In Korea we teach our children to respect museums. They will meet their chaperones at a planned time."

As I watched these children, I remembered my first visit to the United States Holocaust Memorial Museum in Washington, D.C. I was about to begin my tour when several busloads of middle-school students burst into the lobby. They were quite unruly, though there were a number of adults with them. There were several museum docents who attempted to get the students into small groups. They distributed materials and were doing a very good job of explaining the Holocaust and why the United States felt it was important to have this museum in our nation's capital. The students laughed as they passed from exhibit to exhibit. Others who were visiting the museum seemed quite offended by the group. Finally, one chaperone said, "I'm sorry. I don't think they understand." An adult standing in front of one of the exhibits turned to the chaperone and asked, "Why don't they understand?"

I have worked with middle-school students for most of my career, and I know that adolescents laugh when they are uncomfortable. But the blame for that laughter shouldn't be directed at the students. The blame should be directed at those who planned the field trip in the first place. Why didn't they read Lois Lowry's *Number the Stars,* Karen Ackerman's *The Night Crossing,* Carol Matas' *Daniel's Story,* or *Anne Frank: Diary of a Young Girl*? Why didn't they use the nonfiction books that line the shelves of libraries? Books like *Survivors: True Stories of Children in the Holocaust,* by Allan Zullo and Mara Bovsun, and *Hitler Youth: Growing Up in Hitler's Shadow,* by Susan Campbell Bartoletti. Why didn't they discuss these books with the students so that they would have had some knowledge about this tragedy?

At the end of the museum tour a movie was shown, and the students finally got quiet. The thing that silenced them was when Holocaust survivors rolled up their sleeves and revealed their branded numbers. There wasn't an adult present who didn't wish that the movie had been the first thing on the tour.

It's amazing how a trip halfway around the world can point out our failures in working with our own youth. The kids in South Korea were on task

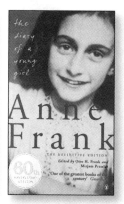
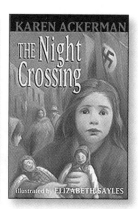

with no hovering adults. Those Korean children wouldn't laugh—they are taught to respect museums, even if they "don't understand." This is why you go to museums. To learn. To eventually understand. And we have libraries filled with books to help us on that journey.

With respect to the middle-school students who were in the Holocaust Memorial Museum that day, I believe they got it in the end. It's too bad someone didn't help them get it before they arrived—I'm sure the docents and other museum attendees would have appreciated it. And I believe that they might even go on to pick up books like *The Book Thief,* by Markus Zusak, *The Boy in the Striped Pajamas,* by John Boyne, and *The Cat with the Yellow Star: Coming of Age in Terezin,* by Susan Goldman Rubin and Ela Weissberger, because of the branded numbers they saw that day. I believe they will read these books because they learned not to laugh.

October 2010

Survivors Club: The True Story of a Very Young Prisoner of Auschwitz. **By Michael Bornstein and Debbie Bornstein Holinstat. 2017. 348p. FSG, $16.99 (9780374305710).**
This narrative nonfiction relates the terror that swept a small Polish village in 1939 when they came under siege from the Nazis and how one family managed to outwit the soldiers and escape a terrible fate at Auschwitz.

TALKING WITH ANGELA CERRITO

**I**n Angela Cerrito's *The Safest Lie,* Anna Bauman is only seven years old when she and her parents are forced to move into a tiny apartment in the Jewish ghetto of Warsaw during World War II. Now she is nine and her family's space has been reduced to a tiny room shared with strangers. They are hungry, cold, and live in constant fear for their safety. Like most of the children in the ghetto, Anna attends Mrs. Rechtman's youth circle. The group distributes clothing and "homework," a code word for food. Then Jolanta, a worker with a Resistance organization, calls upon parents in the ghetto and tells them about a plan to escort their children to safety. This means that the children must be given new names, a new religion, and false papers. Anna is assigned the name Anna Karwolska and is taken to a Catholic orphanage where she stays until she is relocated with a loving Catholic family. She lives this new life not realizing that her foster parents know she is Jewish. Then, at the end of the war, the children with living relatives are forced to once again

give up their homes and return to family they may not even know.

The work of Irena Sendler and other members of the Resistance who made it their mission to deliver the children of the Warsaw Ghetto to safety inspired Cerrito to write this work of fiction. Her research took her to Warsaw, where she had the opportunity to meet and talk with Sendler.

SCALES: In your author's note, you talk about your trip to Warsaw to conduct research for *The Safest Lie.* **What research did you do prior to going to Warsaw?**

CERRITO: I interviewed Mary Skinner by phone. She was working on *Irena Sendler: In the Name of Their Mothers,* a film about Sendler and the child rescues. She also had an English translation of Irena Sendler's biography. I read many books, including Janusz Korczak's *Ghetto Diary* (1978), Gunnar S. Paulsson's *Secret City* (2002), and *The Last Eyewitnesses* (1998), a collection of memoirs. I also frequently checked out the volumes of Lucjan Dobroszycki's *The Chronicles of the Lodz Ghetto* from my local library. While I avoided reading WWII fiction, I did read Korczak's *King Matt the First* (1986), a book my character may have heard as a series of radio broadcasts before the war. Additionally, as part of the Kimberly Colen Memorial Grant, I was able to travel to New York for the Society of Children's Book Writers and Illustrators conference. There I met with Mary Skinner for another interview and toured the Museum of Jewish Heritage and had an opportunity to meet with Ilana Abramovitch.

SCALES: You spent time in the archives of the Jewish Historical Institute in Warsaw. Tell us about specific discoveries you made there that contributed to Anna Bauman's story.

CERRITO: The institute's archives include hundreds of testimonies of children recorded immediately after the war. The translator I worked with, Ewa Prokop, was so shocked, she gasped several times with each account she read. The horrors the children described were so immediate, direct, and matter-of-fact. They told of seeing their family members murdered, as well as being starved and beaten by those entrusted to help them. Even though I'd read a great deal before the trip, I was unprepared. After only a couple of testimonies, it became clear to me that during the war the children's very definition of normal had changed: the fear, the horrific events experienced, day after day—for years, it was their whole world.

This shaped my telling of Anna's story, especially the scene where the printer's children walk to Anna's foster home and tell about the fate of their parents. Additionally, after days of hearing the chilling testimonies, I knew the novel would need balance. I'd already written the scene in the safe house, where Anna is determined to remember her life before the ghetto. After reading the children's testimonies at the institute, I included more of Anna's prewar memories throughout the novel.

SCALES: You also conducted research at the Museum of Jewish History in New York City, and you acknowledge Ilana Abramovitch for offering valuable advice. What kind of advice did you receive from her?

CERRITO: She suggested I look at the big picture rather than become obsessed with small details. She was the second person in two days (the first being author Marvin Terban) who told me my project was likely to grow from the picture book I had planned into a novel. They were correct! Dr. Abramovitch showed me a film clip of an interview with Irena Sendler. In the film, Irena told of another child-rescuer, Anton. This led me to the film *Les Justes*, by Marek Halter. From there I contacted Roissy Films in France and was able to obtain a copy of the film for research. Halter was one of the first to go into Poland and interview typical Polish citizens about their experiences during the war. One of those people was Irena Sendler.

SCALES: Sendler was the inspiration for this novel. Tell us about meeting her.

CERRITO: I felt as if I had been holding my breath for months leading up to meeting Irena, and when I finally stepped into her room, I could exhale. A great deal of planning went into the research trip to Warsaw. Irena was careful not to promise a meeting, only that she would try, and any meeting would depend on how she was feeling—after all, she was 95 years old! The interview was pushed back a day, and I didn't know we would actually meet for certain until an hour before the appointment. She kindly included my friend and my daughter, Alexandria, who was eight years old at the time, in the visit, as well as Ms. Prokop, our translator.

SCALES: Tell us about your conversation.

CERRITO: I asked her about the child rescues and about her friend Eva Rechtman. I told her of the video of her I saw in which she spoke about Anton, and I learned more about Anton's role in the rescues and his fate. We also spoke about her time in prison and about current events, such as the war in the Middle East and Pope John Paul II, who was having health concerns at the time. Throughout our time together, Irena spoke with strength and conviction, often gesturing with her hands and pounding her fist on the armrest of her wheelchair.

SCALES: Did she relate specific details about the children she rescued?

CERRITO: Irena spoke about the child rescues in terms of logistics. She talked about Zegota and being part of the secret organization and spoke often about all of the people who helped her, repeatedly stating, "I didn't do this alone." Speaking of her dear friend Eva Rechtman almost brought her to tears. I was also fortunate to be able to interview Anna Mieskowska, who wrote Irena's authorized biography. Mieskowska had the story behind the story. She knew so many more facts and events that weren't included in her book.

SCALES: It's not surprising to learn that Sendler kept your daughter close by her side during your visit. How did your daughter react to meeting this amazing woman?

CERRITO: The Jewish Historical Institute displayed the temporary exhibit "Children of the Warsaw Ghetto." Alexandria and I saw the exhibit the day before we met Irena. She learned about the conditions in the ghetto where so many children struggled to survive, and about the transports that took thousands of people, including children, to their deaths. She knew who Irena was and that Irena helped children get out of the ghetto. Alexandria was impressed with Irena. She told me, "Her voice was so loud and so strong."

Years later, in high school, Alexandria and her friend did a school presentation about Irena Sendler and the child-rescue operations.

SCALES: At what point did you know that your research was complete and you were ready to write Anna's story?
CERRITO: I think I share this trait with other writers of nonfiction and historical fiction: the research never feels complete. Even through the last draft, I continued to research. During the final draft, on the advice of my editor at Holiday House, Julie Amper, I added more time after the end of the war. Anna was longing for her family to find her. I searched news files and weather reports and added the scene where everyone in town gathers around to listen to the first Polish radio broadcast from Warsaw since the occupation.

SCALES: The novel is told in first person from Anna's point of view. Did you ever consider writing it in third person? How might this have changed the story?
CERRITO: Actually, the very first version was written in third person. It was a completely different novel. I didn't feel as close to Anna. Too much time was spent explaining the changes that were taking place in Poland, rather than showing Anna's and her family's experiences. When I changed to first person, the story felt more immediate and intense. I would say the change of point of view helped me to be Anna.

SCALES: Jolanta and Mrs. Dabrowska represent Irena Sendler. Does Anna embody a bit of Sendler as well?
CERRITO: Jolanta was the code name Irena Sendler used inside the Warsaw Ghetto. She used many aliases after escaping execution, including the name Klara Dabrowska. Anna is forced to hide her identity throughout most of the novel, as Irena did each time she stepped into the ghetto with a fake ID or met with families to arrange care for the children. I think the greatest example of Anna embodying the spirit of Irena is when she enlists Jerzy's help to save Zina and Jozef. Irena never failed to mention that she had a great deal of help with the child rescues. She had to take chances and trust people with

her secrets. She also put herself at risk to save others. The safe thing for Anna would have been to forget about Zina and Jozef. But, like Irena, she couldn't be silent in the face of suffering.

SCALES: When you began the novel, did you plan for Anna to be reunited with her cousin Jakub?

CERRITO: Not initially. In earlier drafts Anna was all alone at the end of the novel. Though this was the typical experience for most rescued children after the war, it tore my heart out each time I read and revised the story. I had to add the reunion with Jakub in order to keep working on the manuscript. I found this was the right thing for the story as well, because it brought me more memories of Anna's childhood and the special relationship she had with Jakub.

SCALES: Why is Anna so surprised to learn that Sophia, Stephan, and Jerzy knew she was Jewish?

CERRITO: From the start, it was a matter of life and death that Anna must never admit her Jewish identity. Though she longed to remember—and be— her true self, she only dared to think about her family and her past when she was alone at night. Though it was obvious to her that the people in the first safe house knew her situation, from the moment she left there, the world knew her as Anna Karwolska. During her time living with Sophia, Stephan, and Jerzy, she always wondered if they would care for her, actually really love her, if they knew her true identity. As she grew to love them, she worried about putting them in danger. At the end of the war, it was a relief to know they knew her secret all along, but also a disappointment. She could have been her true self with them. Similar to Chaim, she hid too well.

SCALES: Young readers will want to know whether Anna ever sees Sophia, Stephan, and Jerzy again. In your mind, are they ever reunited?

CERRITO: Honestly, travel in postwar Poland, especially for those who were Jewish and minors, would have been a challenge. Many children in Anna's situation ended up in refugee camps for years. However, it is nice to imagine that Anna could have brought Jakub to meet her Polish family. If she were able to visit, I'm sure it would have been a happy reunion with fine food and interesting conversation.

SCALES: Children were stripped of their identities in an effort to keep them safe. Chaim was so young when he was rescued that he doesn't believe that he is Jewish. Did you read accounts of children who never reclaimed their identities?

CERRITO: Yes, Anna Mieskowska shared with me stories of several children who were saved by Zegota at such a young age that they had no memory of their true families and true identities. I also read personal accounts in which children were not told about their identities until they were teenagers. Aside from coming as a complete shock, the revelation was often met with disbelief and an enormous sense of loss.

SCALES: Did the title of the novel come to you in the beginning of the writing process or at the end?

CERRITO: The title of this book changed several times. I have to credit the Kehillat Israel School and their webmaster Stephen Rayburn. His website provided me with many ideas for Grandma's sayings. One is "The truth is the safest lie," which inspired the title.

SCALES: What do you feel is the greatest value of historical fiction?

CERRITO: To me the greatest value of historical fiction is that it allows readers to be transported to another time, to be immersed in actual events through the experiences of a character they can relate to and care about.

SCALES: How difficult was it to write *The Safest Lie* after writing a more contemporary novel (*The End of the Line*, 2011)?

CERRITO: Actually, I wrote the first draft of *The Safest Lie* before I had even started writing *The End of the Line*. *The Safest Lie* was more of a challenge because it required more work before it could be published.

SCALES: What are you writing now?

CERRITO: I'm working on a contemporary story about a girl with an unusual talent who will stop at nothing to meet a famous athlete she thinks is a long-lost relative.

FURTHER READING

The following titles about Irena Sendler, the Holocaust, and the rescue of Jewish children make excellent companions to *The Safest Lie.*

A Bag of Marbles. By Joseph Joffo. Illus. by Vincent Bailly. Tr. by Edward Gauvin. 2013. Lerner, $29.27 (9781467707008).
> This graphic novel based on Joffo's 1973 adult memoir tells the story of Jo and his brother as they escape Nazi-occupied Paris in hopes of reuniting with their older brothers on the Italian border. To stay safe, the boys must lose their Jewish identity.

The Cats in Krasinski Square. By Karen Hesse. Illus. by Wendy Watson. 2004. Scholastic, $17.99 (9780439435406).
> In free verse, a young girl tells how she escapes the Warsaw Ghetto and how she and her older sister gather the cats living in Krasinski Square to help them smuggle food and other items to those remaining in the ghetto.

A Hero and the Holocaust: The Story of Janusz Korczak and His Children. By David A. Adler. Illus. by Bill Farnsworth. 2002. Holiday, $16.95 (9780823415489).
> This picture-book biography details the courage of the director of a Polish Jewish orphanage and his efforts to protect the children as they were herded to the Warsaw Ghetto and later to a death camp.

Hiding from the Nazis. By David A. Adler. Illus. by Karen Ritz. 1997. Holiday, $17.95 (9780823412884).
> A Christian family in Holland takes in the daughter of German Jewish refugees and protects her from the Nazis, but when the war is over and her parents come for her, the child has become so attached to her new family that she doesn't want to leave.

In My Hands: Memories of a Holocaust Rescuer. By Irene Gut Opdyke and Jennifer Armstrong. 1999. Knopf, $10.99 (9780553538847).
> Irene Gut was a 17-year-old Polish nursing student when she bravely saved the lives of at least 12 Jews in Nazi-occupied Poland.

Irena Sendler: Bringing Life to Children of the Holocaust. By Susan Brophy Down. 2012. illus. Crabtree, $33.27 (9780778725565).
> Irena Sendler was only 17 when she devised a plan, including smuggling

a small baby in a toolbox, that saved thousands of Jewish children during the Holocaust.

Irena Sendler and the Children of the Warsaw Ghetto. **By Susan Goldman Rubin. Illus. by Bill Farnsworth. 2011. Holiday, $16.20 (9780823422517).**
This is another nicely detailed account of Sendler's rescue campaign.

Irena's Jars of Secrets. **By Marcia Vaughan. Illus. by Ron Mazellan. 2011. Lee & Low, $11.44 (9781600604393).**
This picture-book biography provides an introduction to the humanitarian work of Irena Sendler, focusing on her efforts to record the names of the children from the Warsaw Ghetto so that they might be reunited with their parents.

Mister Doctor: Janusz Korczak and the Orphans of the Warsaw Ghetto. **By Irene Cohen-Janca. Illus. by Maurizio A. C. Quarello. 2015. Annick, $24.95 (9781554517152).**
This account is based on the true story of an orphanage director in Poland who refused to leave the children when they were taken to the Warsaw Ghetto. His story led the United Nations to adopt the Declaration of the Rights of the Child in 1959.

A free and extensive Educator's Guide on *The Safest Lie* is available on the Holiday House website: http://holidayhouse.com/docs/SafestLie_EdGuide_HiRes.pdf.

September 2015

The Dollmaker of Krakow. **By R. M. Romer. 2017. 336p. Delacorte, $16.99 (9781524715397).**
A dollmaker in Poland works for the Resistance and uses magic to smuggle children from the Jewish Ghetto in Krakow to safe houses outside the city.

Genevieve's War. **By Patricia Reilly Giff. 2017. 240p. Holiday House, $16.95 (9780823438006).**
Set in 1939 in occupied France, Genevieve, an American girl, is with her grandmother on her farm in Alsace when things become very dangerous. A Nazi officer takes over a room in the farmhouse, and Genevieve discovers that her beloved brother is working for the Resistance.

NO ONE
WANTED US

n my city, there is a bronze statue on Main Street of a beloved former mayor, Max Heller, who was a Holocaust survivor. In 1998, he and his wife taped their stories for the oral-history library at the United States Holocaust Memorial Museum. I recently had the pleasure of visiting with his 93-year-old widow, Trude Heller, over lunch, and she says that she sees her life as a series of miracles. Born in Vienna, she was an only child, and very sheltered. One day she went to gym class in a city that was considered very safe, and when she came out, there were swastikas everywhere. That was in 1938. Her father's business was destroyed during Kristallnacht, and the family was given six hours to vacate their spacious apartment and move to the ghetto. Nazis came to arrest her father, but neighbors hid him. And Trude and her mother began a long journey to Antwerp, Belgium, where they lived with refugee status for a year because no country would take them. "No one wanted us," Trude recalls.

Trude and her husband devoted their lives to humanitarian issues, and she still goes to middle schools and talks about the Holocaust. She connects issues such as bullying to Hitler and the Nazi Party, advising students to think about the direction bullying could take them. She urges them and everyone to "listen to the stories of Holocaust survivors" and "listen to the stories of refugees."

The news today is filled with stories of Syrian refugees, and political candidates—and others—are heatedly arguing about whether the United States should allow vetted refugees into the country. As I listened to Trude Heller's story, I couldn't help but think that history is repeating itself: "No one wanted us."

But history is full of refugee stories, and libraries are filled with novels and true accounts of their plight: *Number the Stars* (1989), by Lois Lowry; *When Hitler Stole Pink Rabbit* (1997), by Judith Kerr; and *A Faraway Island* (2009), by Annika Thor and Linda Schenck are just a few examples of Holocaust refugee stories. L. S. Matthews' *Fish* (2006), the story of a family's escape from their adopted unnamed country, could be set in a number of war-torn countries where the lives of natives and humanitarian workers are in danger. Sudanese refugees are depicted in *Of Beetles and Angels: A Boy's Remarkable Journey from a Refugee Camp to Harvard* (2002), by Mawi Asgedom; *Brothers in Hope* (2005), by Mary Williams; *Home of the Brave* (2007), by Katherine Applegate; *A Long Walk to Water* (2010), by Linda Sue Park; and *The Red Pencil* (2014), by Andrea Davis Pinkney; Kosovo refugees in *Drita, My Homegirl* (2006), by Jenny Lombard, and *The Day of the Pelican* (2009), by Katherine Paterson. In *Children of the River* (1991), by Linda Crew, Sundara flees Cambodia with her aunt's family and takes refuge in the

United States; and *Goodbye, Vietnam* (1992), by Gloria Whelan, shows one Vietnamese family's terrifying escape from their homeland to Hong Kong. And then there's Malala Yousafzai, perhaps the most famous young refugee today. She tells her story in *I Am Malala: How One Girl Stood Up for Education and Changed the World* (2014).

Recently, I saw a picture of Anne Frank alongside a caption that reads, "Anne Frank's visa application was turned down by the United States government." And I think of Trude Heller's story and her "series of miracles": the miracle that she escaped Vienna before the Nazis built concentration camps for women; the miracle that united her with her husband, Max; and the miracle that brought them to my city. He became a favorite son of that city, and she a great First Lady. At one point, she returned to Vienna for a brief visit. When she passed through immigration on her way back to the United States, the officer, noting her birth city, said, "Oh, you've come home." She replied, "No, I'm going home." This, too, could be the response of refugee children or teens today—if only someone wanted them.

January 2016

Stormy Seas: Stories of Young Boat Refugees. **By Mary Beth Leatherdale. Illus. by Eleanor Shakespeare. 2017. 64p. Annick, $24.95 (9781554518968).**
  Five teen refugees forced to leave their homes due to war are profiled with interviews, photos, and key historical information. Ruth escapes Nazi Germany, Phu is forced to leave Vietnam, José leaves Cuba, Najeeba escapes the Taliban in Afghanistan, and Mohamed is the victim of human traffickers before settling in Italy.

Refugee. **By Alan Gratz. 2017. 338p. Scholastic, $16.99 (9780545880831).**
  In this work of fiction, Josef, a Jewish boy, flees Nazi Germany in the 1930s; Isabel, a Cuban girl, escapes her dangerous country on a raft in 1994; and Mahmoud, a Syrian boy, seeks refuge in Europe in 2015.

TALKING WITH
SUSAN GOLDMAN RUBIN

 **oung readers study the civil rights movement in** school. Most may know something about the March on Washington, Bloody Sunday, the Montgomery bus boycott, and the bombing of the Sixteenth Street Baptist Church in Birmingham, Alabama. They learn about Martin Luther King Jr., his dynamic leadership, and his dedication to nonviolence on his long journey to gain civil rights for African Americans in the South. Students know about Rosa Parks and her contribution to the movement, and some have heard of the Little Rock Nine. But few have heard of Freedom Summer. They don't know because many American history textbooks and trade books for youth about the civil rights movement give little attention to the events that occurred in Mississippi in the summer of 1964.

Now young readers have a new opportunity to learn about this important chapter of the civil rights movement, because Susan Goldman Rubin has written a powerful account of it. Known for her nonfiction works that focus on human rights issues, Rubin approaches *Freedom Summer: The 1964 Struggle for Civil Rights in Mississippi* (2014) with passion and a commitment to make these events as significant and real as the marches, the bombings, and the sit-ins. The source notes reveal her meticulous attention to detail and her dedication to uncovering the truth. She presents facts with clarity and honesty while also telling a powerful story. The book is arranged by date, beginning in June 1964, when the volunteers arrived in the Mississippi delta, and ending in late August, when they departed. Maps of Mississippi, black-and-white photographs, and drawings created by participants document the activities of the summer volunteers and the people they came to serve. There are expressions of

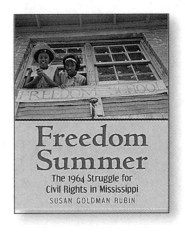

despair and fear, but there is also joy, a sense of hope, and an urgency to complete the task.

Readers will know after reading Rubin's book that the Student Nonviolent Coordinating Committee (SNCC), a civil rights group that grew out of the lunch counter sit-ins in the early 1960s, organized Freedom Summer. This group called upon college students from across the country to go to Mississippi and register African Americans to vote and to establish Freedom Schools to educate adults and their children. Though some African Americans were too frightened to participate, many opened their homes to white volunteers. Elected officials and law enforcement in Mississippi felt that this was an overt disregard of the state's segregation laws. Hostilities erupted, and threats became a daily occurrence. After three volunteers disappeared and were ultimately assumed to have been murdered, people became more anxious. But most participants didn't allow fear to interrupt their work. No one was more determined than Fannie Lou Hamer, an African American woman who had helped the SNCC organize the groundwork in Mississippi. She was elected vice chair of the Mississippi Freedom Democratic Party, attended the 1964 Democratic Convention, and continued to be a voice for voter rights for the remainder of her life. Rubin dedicates Freedom Summer to the memory of Mrs. Hamer and her followers.

Summer 2014 marked the fiftieth anniversary of Freedom Summer. Readers of all ages may continue to commemorate this occasion by learning about the Mississippi Summer Project through Rubin's book. When people know the facts and, through Rubin's account, meet those who made it all happen, then Freedom Summer may finally occupy its rightful place in the history books. In the conversation below, Rubin talks about her motivation for writing the book, her extensive research, and her unwavering dedication to reveal the events exactly as they occurred.

SCALES: There are a few books for young readers that provide encyclopedic information about Freedom Summer, but your book allows readers to connect to the people, their passion for their mission, and the sacrifices they made. How did you decide to write about Freedom Summer?

RUBIN: My editor, Mary Cash, knew that I was interested in the civil rights movement. She asked me if I wanted to do a book on Freedom Summer. I vaguely remembered the events of 1964 when three civil rights workers were killed. I mistakenly thought that Andrew Goodman, one of three, had gone to Oberlin College, my alma mater. I had graduated in 1959, and many of my friends were actively involved in the civil rights movement. The murders had greatly disturbed me. I wanted to know what actually happened and thought that this was an important period to research and write about. I discovered that few people knew much about it, even those who were well read, yet it was a turning point in American history. I also wanted to pay tribute to leaders in the civil rights movement whose names were not well known: Mrs. Fannie Lou Hamer, Bob Moses, Charles McLaurin, Leslie McLemore, Lawrence Guyot, and Dave Dennis.

SCALES: Tell us about your research process. What was your first source, and where did it lead you?

RUBIN: I started by reading a few books on Freedom Summer written for adults. I learned that many of the Freedom Summer volunteers came from Oberlin, so I contacted the Oberlin Alumni Association. I learned that an article had just been written for the alumni magazine about Oberlin alumni who had participated in the civil rights movement in the early 1960s. I contacted the author of the article, E. J. Dickson, and she put me in touch with people she had interviewed. One of the first I wrote to was Matthew Rinaldi. He gave me an extensive reading list and names of others I should contact. One interview led to another. Martha Honey, another Oberlin alum, told me about Tracy Sugarman, an older artist and writer who had gone to Mississippi intending to observe and record but had wound up participating as well as publishing accounts of his experiences. I had the wonderful opportunity of talking to him by telephone shortly before he died. I was about to receive the Carter G. Woodson Book Award for my book about Leonard Bernstein (*Music Was It: Young Leonard Bernstein*, 2011), and the presentation was to be at the meeting of the Social Studies Council in Seattle. Rita Schwerner Bender—the widow of Mickey Schwerner, one of the three who was killed—is a lawyer in Seattle. When I wrote to her asking to see her and told her why I would be in Seattle, she agreed to talk to me. That meeting set me on the right track for focusing my research on Mississippians and the work still to be done.

SCALES: You say in the book that an important part of your research was the time you spent in Mississippi. How did the people receive you?
RUBIN: They were warm and wonderful, wanting me to tell this story to readers. Thanks to a helpful former Freedom Summer volunteer, Linda Davis, I got in touch with Stacy White, in Indianola, Mississippi. Stacy had been in charge of previous reunions of the volunteers. It was her great-aunt, Irene Magruder, who had been the first African American in Mississippi to host Freedom Summer volunteers. Stacy became my new friend and guide. Through e-mails and phone conversations, we planned my trip to Jackson and Indianola. With her help, I arranged a meeting with Dr. Leslie McLemore at the Hamer Institute on the campus of Jackson State University. I interviewed Charles McLaurin, a veteran of the civil rights movement who I had read about in books, and he took me on a tour of important sites in the delta. Stacy and another former volunteer, Margaret Kibbee, drove me around Greenwood to see where events had taken place. Stacy invited me to a monthly meeting of the Sunflower County Civil Rights Organization, in Indianola, and I learned more about ongoing problems and concerns.

SCALES: What did you find in Mississippi that you couldn't find in books?
RUBIN: I found out that there is still a struggle for racial equality. Many people live in terrible conditions. Programs have been set up to help prepare

African American children academically to meet standards and qualify for college so that they can become leaders in the community. But these children still have to fight for better education in public schools. I visited the Sunflower County Freedom Project, which was inspired by the Freedom Schools set up in 1964. I met some of the students who are involved in the after-school program, and they told me about the different classes they're taking, everything from fitness and hip-hop to reading American novels and performing in original plays about their own history.

SCALES: How do you know when your research is complete and you are ready to write the book?

RUBIN: It helped to have a deadline. We knew we wanted this book to be published in spring 2014, in time for the fiftieth anniversary of Freedom Summer. Yet I kept coming across new information that I thought was vital. Up till the last minute, my editor encouraged me to add stories about my visit to Mississippi and the archival material that I found there. Everyone at Holiday House worked like mad to bring the book out on time. The research is never complete. I keep reading new articles in the paper and seeing documentaries that add fresh information. That's what makes nonfiction so exciting. It's an ongoing study.

SCALES: The book is organized by date. How did you decide that this timeline approach was the best way to chronicle the summer events?

RUBIN: From experience, I knew that readers prefer a chronological sequence in a work of nonfiction. I wanted this to be a page-turner: suspenseful, yet accurate to the best of my ability, based on secondary and primary research. I looked for the narrative line. The story had to begin and end with Freedom Summer, but I needed an additional chapter that we titled "Aftermath" to let readers know how the killers were finally identified and stood trial.

SCALES: The photographs greatly contribute to the story. Were you involved in selecting the photographs and the placement of them within the text?

RUBIN: I chose just about all of the photographs we used. I had gained enthusiastic permission from Tracy Sugarman to use his drawings for the book when we talked on the phone before he died. And I discovered many marvelous snapshots taken by Freedom Summer volunteers during their stay in Mississippi. Mary Cash and her valiant assistant, Kelly Loughman, brought some photos to my attention. I often had to track down the source of the photographs to gain high-resolution images and negotiate permission fees to reproduce the pictures. In the process, I talked with some of the photographers who had actually been there during Freedom Summer. One of the most difficult photos to find and use was the one on the cover, by Ken Thompson, who died years ago. The story of how we finally found it is a story in itself and would take a whole article to tell. I suggested places where some of the images could go, but the layout was largely the work of the dedicated design team at Holiday House.

SCALES: In your mind, is there an iconic photograph that speaks to the triumphs and sacrifices of those involved with Freedom Summer?

RUBIN: Oh, that's a very difficult choice. Of course, the FBI missing poster with the photos of Andrew Goodman, James Earl Chaney, and Mickey Schwerner tells it all. Herbert Randall's photos of children reading in the Freedom Library and of the Palmer's Crossing Community Center and Pete Seeger performing there reveal so much. Voter registration canvassing with Dick Landerman sitting on the porch of Hattiesburg resident Horace Laurence tells another part of the story. I'm grateful that we could use as many images as we did in *Freedom Summer*.

SCALES: Your book has now given Fannie Lou Hamer a special spot in the history books. Children will come away from *Freedom Summer* with the

knowledge that she was an important personality in the civil rights movement. What else should children know about Mrs. Hamer?

RUBIN: She continued to fight for civil rights and social change. Even after the Voting Rights Act was passed in 1965, the Mississippi legislature and many of the state's counties were making African Americans re-register to vote. Mrs. Hamer worked on voter education projects. At that time, there were few African

Americans holding office in Sunflower County, and she kept talking about the need for change. She advocated rights for women of color. Building on the success of the Freedom Summer schools, she became involved in Head Start programs in Mississippi. To combat poverty, she started Freedom Farm, a cooperative where people could grow and pick their own crops. Infant mortality was almost cut in half as poor people, white and black, ate better food. She opened a day care center for the children of women working at a garment factory that she had established to provide jobs. Mrs. Hamer's humanitarian efforts deserve a new book for children. I want to know more about her. She died in 1977, having spent all of her strength and her meager savings to help others.

SCALES: In the book's epilogue, civil rights veteran Charles McLaurin says, "The Movement never stops." What are the civil rights issues today that children need to think about?

RUBIN: Children need to think about racism in America and help make changes. They need to think about the vote as a right and responsibility. There are renewed obstacles for African Americans to overcome in order to register to vote. Education, including reading and math skills, is absolutely necessary before an 18-year-old can cast an informed vote about issues that will affect his or her life for the better. Yet public education is not equal in many states, especially in parts of Mississippi. Programs such as the Sunflower County Freedom Project have been established to prepare public school students to qualify for college and leadership roles. But poverty is a big problem. Mississippi is the poorest state in the U.S. and needs help for the children.

SCALES: What is your next project?

RUBIN: My next books are about figures in the arts. *Stand There! She Shouted: The Invincible Photographer Julia Margaret Cameron* is due out in fall 2014, and I'm finishing work on the forthcoming *Putting It Together: The Musical Theater of Stephen Sondheim* and *Hot Pink: The Life and Fashions of Elsa Schiaparelli*. And I am also starting a biography of architect and artist Maya Lin, who designed the Vietnam Veterans Memorial.

SAMPLING GOLDMAN RUBIN

Andy Warhol: Pop Art Painter. 2006. 48p. illus. Abrams, $19.95
(9780810954779).

The Anne Frank Case: Simon Wiesenthal's Search for the Truth. Illus. by Bill
Farnsworth. 2009. 40p. Holiday, $18.95 (9780823421091); paper, $8.95
(9780823423088).

The Cat with the Yellow Star: Coming of Age in Terezin. By Susan Goldman
Rubin and Ela Weissberger. 2006. 40p. illus.
Holiday, $17.95 (9780823418312).

Delicious: The Life and Art of Wayne Thiebaud.
2007. 104p. illus. Chronicle, $15.95
(9780811851688).

Diego Rivera: An Artist for the People. 2013. 56p.
illus. Abrams, $21.95 (9780810984110).

*Everybody Paints! The Lives and Art of the Wyeth
Family.* 2014. 112p. illus. Chronicle, $16.99
(9780811869843).

*The Flag with Fifty-Six Stars: A Gift from the Sur-
vivors of Matthausen.* Illus. by Bill Farnsworth. 2005. 40p. Holiday, $17.95
(9780823416530); paper, $6.95 (9780823420193).

Freedom Summer: The 1964 Struggle for Civil Rights in Mississippi. 2014. 128p.
illus. Holiday, $18.95 (9780823429202).

Irena Sendler and the Children of the Warsaw Ghetto. Illus. by Bill Farnsworth. 2011. 40p. Holiday, $18.95 (9780823422517); paper, $8.99
(9780823425952).

Jean Lafitte: The Pirate Who Saved America. Illus. by Jeff Himmelman. 2012.
48p. Abrams, $18.95 (9780810997332).

Music Was It: Young Leonard Bernstein. 2011. 192p. illus. Charlesbridge, $19.95
(9781580893442).

*Stand There! She Shouted: The Invincible Photographer Julia Margaret
Cameron.* Illus. by Bagram Ibatoulline. 2014. 80p. Candlewick, $16.99
(9780763657536).

Whaam! The Art and Life of Roy Lichtenstein. 2008. 48p. illus. Abrams, $19.95
(9780810994928).

Wideness and Wonder: The Life and Art of Georgia O'Keeffe. 2011. 112p. illus.
Chronicle, $16.99 (9780811869836).

The following titles about the civil rights movement make excellent companions to Susan Goldman Rubin's *Freedom Summer: The 1964 Struggle for Civil
Rights in Mississippi.*

FICTION

Freedom School, Yes! By Amy Littlesugar. Illus. by Floyd Cooper. 2001. 40p. Philomel, $16.99 (9780399230066).

> In Chicken Creek, Mississippi, Jolie, a young black narrator, relates what happens when her family houses a white Freedom School teacher in the summer of 1964 and how the teacher makes a difference in her life.

Freedom Summer. By Deborah Wiles. Illus. by Jerome Lagarrigue. 2001; reprinted 2014. 32p. Atheneum, $17.99 (9781481422987); Aladdin, paper, $7.99 (9780689878299).

> In the South in the summer just after the passage of the 1964 Civil Rights Act, a black boy and a white boy forge a friendship and come face-to-face with racism.

Glory Be. By Augusta Scattergood. 2012. 208p. Scholastic, $16.99 (9780545331807); e-book, $16.99 (9780545452328).

> In Hanging Moss, Mississippi, in 1964, 11-year-old Gloriana Hemphill, the daughter of a widowed preacher, hasn't noticed the racial injustices in her town until she meets a girl from the North who points them out to her.

Revolution. By Deborah Wiles. 2014. 544p. Scholastic, $19.99 (9780545106078); e-book, $19.99 (9780545634007).

> It's 1964, and Sunny feels as though her life has been invaded when civil rights workers come to her town of Greenwood, Mississippi, to register blacks to vote. As the summer progresses, she learns about the Summer Project and discovers her own voice in the debate.

NONFICTION

The 1964 Freedom Summer. By Rebecca Felix. 2014. 112p. illus. ABDO, lib. ed., $34.22 (9781624032561); e-book, $34.22 (9781624018329).

> The eight chapters of this Essential Events series title outline the events of Freedom Summer and include eyewitness accounts of the violence that erupted, those who survived, and the changes created by the Summer Project, not only in Mississippi but throughout the South.

The Civil Rights Act of 1964: Landmark Antidiscrimination Legislation. **By Susan Wright. 2005. 48p. illus. Rosen, lib. ed., $29.25 (9781404204553).**

>Part of the Library of American Laws and Legal Principles series, this brief and simple overview presents three major topics: the need for the Civil Rights Act, the civil rights movement, and enforcement of the act.

Extraordinary People of the Civil Rights Movement. **By Sheila Hardy and P. Stephen Hardy. 2007. 288p. illus. Children's Press, o.p.**

>Leaders, such as Fannie Lou Hamer, and major events, including the 1964 Summer Project in Mississippi, are briefly covered in this Extraordinary People series volume that chronicles the civil rights movement from 1954 to 1968.

Freedom Summer. **By David Aretha. 2007. 128p. illus. Morgan Reynolds, lib. ed., $28.95 (9781599350592). 323.1196.**

>This entry in the Civil Rights Movement series chronicles the summer of 1964, when the Student Nonviolent Coordinating Committee conducted the project in Mississippi to register blacks to vote.

The Freedom Summer Murders. **By Don Mitchell. 2014. 256p. illus. Scholastic, $18.99 (9780545477253); e-book, $18.99 (9780545633932).**

>Full of original research and interviews with many personally involved, this book goes into detail about the murder of three civil rights workers in Mississippi during the summer of 1964 and how the perpetrators were brought to at least partial justice.

Heroes for Civil Rights. **By David A. Adler. Illus. by Bill Farnsworth. 2008. 32p. Holiday, lib. ed., $17.95 (9780823420087).**

>The one-page biographical information on each of the featured heroes focuses on their important roles in advancing social justice and includes people like Fannie Lou Hamer and her part in the 1964 Freedom Summer Project.

A History of Voting Rights. **By Tamra Orr. 2012. 48p. illus. Mitchell Lane, lib. ed., $29.95 (9781612282626); e-book, $29.95 (9781612283395).**

>The history of how minority groups—blacks, women, and Native Americans—fought to gain the right to vote is presented in this Vote America series volume and includes a discussion about the current issues related to voter suppression and the Latino vote.

Inspiring African American Civil Rights Leaders. **By Stephen Feinstein. 2012. 112p. illus. Enslow, lib. ed., $31.93 (9781598451368); paper, $9.95 (9781464400353).**

>The profiles of eight civil rights leaders in this African American Collective biography include Fannie Lou Hamer.

James Forman and the SNCC. By Michael V. Uschan. 2013. 112p. illus. Lucent,
lib. ed., $34.80 (9781420509205).

> This Library of Black History series title discusses the purpose and work
> of the Student Nonviolent Coordinating Committee and includes a chapter
> that specifically deals with their work with voter registration in the South.

Let It Shine: Stories of Black Women Freedom Fighters. By Andrea
Davis Pinkney. Illus. by Stephen Alcorn. 2000. 120p. Houghton, $20
(9780152010058); paper, $9.99 (9780547906041).

> These real-life stories include well-known black women like Harriet
> Tubman, Sojourner Truth, and Rosa Parks, but there are also stories about
> women, such as Fannie Lou Hamer, who played an important role in the
> civil rights movement.

The "Mississippi Burning" Civil Rights Murder Conspiracy Trial. By Harvey Fireside. 2002. 112p. illus. Enslow, o.p.

> The legal corruption in Mississippi caused the Supreme Court to order
> that the trial of the men accused of the deaths of three Freedom Summer
> volunteers be tried in federal court. This book examines the trial and the
> convictions of these murderers.

Murder in Mississippi: The 1964 Freedom Summer Killings. By Stephen Currie.
2006. 104p. illus. Lucent, $36.95 (9781590189344).

> A Crime Scene Investigation Laboratory Manual series title, this examina-
> tion of the murders of three civil rights workers—Andrew Goodman,
> James Earl Chaney, and Michael Schwerner—in Mississippi in 1964 gives
> details of how FBI agents finally became involved and how they
> approached the investigation.

Oh, Freedom! Kids Talk about the Civil Rights Move-
ment with the People Who Made It Happen. By
Casey King and Linda Barrett Osborne. Illus. by
Joe Brooks. 1997. 144p. Random, paper, $12.95
(9780679890058).

> This oral history project, conducted by
> fourth-graders, presents short interviews with
> people who lived through the civil rights move-
> ment and is divided into three sections: "Life
> under Segregation," "The Movement to End Legalized Segregation," and
> "The Struggle to End Poverty and Discrimination."

Selma and the Voting Rights Act. By David Aretha. 2007. 128p. illus. Morgan
Reynolds, lib. ed., $28.95 (9781599350561).

> Violence and lack of support from the government and local law enforce-
> ment ended the 1964 Freedom Summer Project in Mississippi, and atten-

tion turned to Selma, Alabama, in early 1965, where 99 percent of the voters were white. This book is part of the publisher's Civil Rights Movement series.

When Thunder Comes: Poems for Civil Rights Leaders. By J. Patrick Lewis. Illus. by Jim Burke and others. 2012. 44p. Chronicle, $16.99 (9781452101194); e-book, $16.89 (9781452119441).

These poems about civil- and human-rights activists include ones about James Earl Chaney, Andrew Goodman, and Michael Schwerner, the three civil rights volunteers who were murdered in Mississippi in the summer of 1964.

A free and extensive Educator's Guide for Rubin's book is available on the Holiday House website: https://www.holidayhouse.com/docs/FreeSummer Final_LoRes.pdf.

September 2014

LOVING V. VIRGINIA AND INTERRACIAL FAMILIES

ildred Jeter, a black woman, and Richard Loving, a white man, were married in Washington, DC, on July 11, 1955. Five weeks later, they were arrested at their home in Virginia because the law made interracial marriage illegal in their state. They moved back to DC, where their marriage was recognized, and began a nine-year legal battle to make it lawful in Virginia. The case wound up in the U.S. Supreme Court in 1967, where it was ruled unanimously that prohibiting interracial marriage was unconstitutional. Today, *Loving v. Virginia* is known as one of the landmark civil rights cases and was cited as the precedent in the 2015 same-sex marriage case.

Selina Alko's picture book *The Case for Loving* (2015), illustrated by Selina Alko and Sean Qualls, tells the story of the Lovings and their fight to have their love recognized. The couple had three children—Donald, Peggy, and Sidney—but there were no children's book characters that looked like them. The books included here celebrate interracial families. In some of the books, the characters struggle with being biracial, but for most, it is simply who they are.

BIBLIOGRAPHY

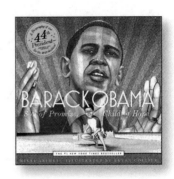

Barack Obama: Son of Promise, Child of Hope. **By Nikki Grimes. Illus. by Bryan Collier. 2008. Simon & Schuster, $16.99 (9781416971443).**

> This picture-book biography of Barack Obama reveals how his white mother and grandmother gave him hope in the absence of his Kenyan father. Though his parents got divorced, both inspired him to find hope in education, and he learned to confront racism and was moved to help the poor.

Black Is Brown Is Tan. **By Arnold Adoff. Illus. by Emily Arnold McCully. 2002. Harper, $17.99 (9780060287764).**

> Complete with new illustrations, this is an updated version of Adoff's 1973 picture-book poem, which was the first children's book about an interracial family. life. Adoff's 1960 marriage to children's author Virginia Hamilton violated segregation laws in 28 states, and he references this poem as an "enduring song" to their now-adult children.

Black, White, Just Right! **By Marguerite W. Davol. Illus. by Irene Trivas. 1993. Albert Whitman, $16.99 (9780807507858).**

> A biracial child is loved and happy and made to feel "just right!" in a family that celebrates their differences and the things they love. Double-page spreads show how members of the family are individuals with likes and dislikes, hobbies, and habits that move beyond stereotypes.

The Blossoming Universe of Violet Diamond. **By Brenda Woods. 2014. Penguin/Nancy Paulsen, $16.99 (9780399257148).**

> The daughter of a white mother and black father, eleven-year-old Violet often feels like an outsider and wonders about her father, who was killed in a car accident when she was an infant. She gains a better sense of self after meeting her father's mother, who manages to answer some of Violet's burning questions.

Brendan Buckley's Universe and Everything in It. **By Sundee T. Frazier. 2007. Delacorte, $6.99 (9780440422068).**

> Mixed-race Brendan, ten years old and a science lover, knows the mother of his black father, but he has never met the estranged father of his white

mother. One day, Brendan meets his white grandfather at a rock club meeting, and the two form a bond, which they manage to keep a secret until a tragedy changes everything.

Cinnamon Baby. By Nicola Winstanley. Illus. by Janice Nadeau. 2011. Kids Can, $16.95 (9781553378211).

Miriam the baker sings as she kneads spices into the dough of her cinnamon bread. The scents and songs attract bicyclist Sebastian. Eventually, they have a beautiful new baby who cries continuously—until Miriam makes a batch of cinnamon bread. Miriam is paper white, Sebastian is cocoa brown, and their cinnamon-colored child gives the title a sly double meaning.

The Hello, Goodbye Window. By Norton Juster. Illus. by Chris Raschka. 2005. Hyperion, $18.99 (9780786809141).

The simple text and impressionistic mixed-media illustrations tell the story of a loving interracial family. The young narrator visits her grandparents, Nanna and Poppy, in their big house.

Hope. By Isabell Monk. Illus. by Janice Lee Porter. 1999. Carolrhoda, o.p.

Hope, a biracial child, is in the second grade when someone asks her if she is "mixed." Aunt Poogie tells her the story of her heritage and her name, and assures her that she is "mixed" with love. In the sequel, *Family* (2001), Hope attends a family reunion on Aunt Poogie's farm.

In Our Mothers' House. By Patricia Polacco. Illus. by the author. 2009. Philomel, o.p.

The oldest of three adopted children recalls her childhood with mothers Marmee and Meema, as they raised their African American daughter, Asian American son, and Caucasian daughter in a lively, supportive neighborhood. Filled with recollections of family holidays, rituals, and special moments, each memory reveals loving insight.

Mixed Me! By Taye Diggs. Illus. by Shane W. Evans. 2015. Feiwel & Friends, $17.99 (9781250047199).

Diggs and Evans follow *Chocolate Me!* (2011) with another joyful story about embracing who you are. Told in rhyming verse, a biracial boy learns to deal with questions and stares from people he encounters and proudly explains that his daddy has black skin and his mother white.

More More More, Said the Baby. By Vera B. Williams. Illus. by the author. 1990. Greenwillow, $17.99 (9780688091736).

A Caldecott Honor Book, this includes three vignettes about the love of three diverse families. The three toddlers—nicknamed Little Guy, Little

Pumpkin, and Little Bird—are a white child, a biracial child, and an Asian American child, and this playful, multiracial, and multi-generational classic is full of affection.

My Two Grannies. By Floella Benjamin. Illus. by Margaret Chamberlain. 2009. Frances Lincoln, $7.95 (9781847800343).

Being biracial isn't a problem for Alvina, and she loves her two fun-loving grannies, one from Trinidad and the other from Yorkshire, England. Things get a little out of control for Alvina when her grannies come to babysit while her parents are away, but she comes up with a clever plan to make their time together more pleasant.

One Word from Sophia. By Jim Averbeck. Illus. by Yasmeen Ismail. 2015. Atheneum, $17.99 (9781481405140).

Sophia wants a giraffe for her birthday, and she carefully appeals to each member of her interracial family. Approaching each family member individually, Sophia cleverly tailors her presentation to fit her audience, offering evidence to her mother, who is a judge, and a business plan to her businessman father. Sophia is told she is too effusive, too verbose, and too loquacious, until she tries a single word: please.

The Other Half of My Heart. By Sundee T. Frazier. 2010. 306p. Delacorte, $16.99 (9780385734400).

Eleven-year-old Minni and Keira are biracial twins, but Minni's coloring is close to their white father, while Keira resembles their black mother. When they go to visit their grandmother in North Carolina, they are entered into a beauty contest for African Americans, but some question whether Minni qualifies.

The Road to Paris. By Nikki Grimes. 2006. Putnam, $16.99 (9780399245374).

In clear, short chapters, Grimes follows nine-year-old biracial Paris Richmond, who is placed in a foster home because her African American mother abuses alcohol, and her white father is unknown. Paris deals with a great deal of bigotry in her new white neighborhood and begins to wonder if she will ever fit in.

Violet. By Tania Duprey Stehlik. Illus. by Vanja Vuleta Jovanovic. 2009. Second Story, $15.95 (9781897187609).

Violet is worried because she looks different from other students at her new school. Her mother is red and her dad blue, and she doesn't understand why she is purple. But when her mother uses paint to show her what happens when red is mixed with blue, Violet is satisfied. In a happy ending to this allegorical tale, she soon finds that her friends don't care that she is different.

The World of Daughter McGuire. By Sharon Dennis Wyeth. 2001. Delacorte, $12 (9780375895029).

In this humorous novel, eleven-year-old Daughter has just enrolled in a new school, where she spends most of her time avoiding troublemakers like the Avengers (a would-be gang with a juvenile-delinquent leader), who call mixed-race Daughter a "zebra." Things get complicated when her teacher assigns a family heritage project, because, as everyone knows, Daughter's family is all mixed up: "African-Italian-Irish-Jewish-Russian-American."

FURTHER RESOURCES: THE LOVINGS

Books

The Case for Loving: The Fight for Interracial Marriage. By Selina Alko. Illus. by Sean Qualls and Selina Alko. 2015. Scholastic, $18.99 (9780545478533).

Loving vs. Virginia: A Documentary Novel of the Landmark Civil Rights Case. By Patricia Hruby Powell. Illus. by Shadra Strickland. 2017. Chronicle, $21.99 (9781452125909).

Loving v. Virginia: Lifting the Ban against Interracial Marriage. By Susan Dudley Gold. 2007. Cavendish, o.p.

Websites

www.encyclopediavirginia.org/loving_v_virginia_1967

www.biography.com/people/mildred-loving-5884

www.npr.org/templates/story/story.php?storyId=10889047

IN THE CLASSROOM

- Loving Day is celebrated annually on June 12, the anniversary of the Supreme Court decision in the *Loving v. Virginia* case. Discuss all kinds of families and then have readers develop an annotated bibliography of books about different kinds of families as suggested reading for Loving Day.

- Mildred Loving died in 2008, before same-sex marriage was legalized. Ask older readers to write an essay, or prepare a speech that explains why Mildred Loving became a champion for same-sex marriage.

- Read aloud *The Case for Loving* and *In Our Mothers' House* (Polacco). Engage readers with the following discussion questions::
  - » Compare the family in Polacco's story to that of the Lovings. How is love celebrated in both families?
  - » How do you know that the children in both stories respect their parents?
  - » Tell readers that, in the field of law, a precedent is a rule established in an earlier case. Explain why *Loving v. Virginia* was the precedent for the same-sex-marriage case in 2015. Ask them to discuss the meaning of civil rights. How were the decisions in these two cases victories for civil rights?

January 2017

TROUBLE, FOLKS

ight here in River City.

I was in high school when my parents took me to Birmingham, Alabama, to see the traveling performance of Meredith Wilson's *The Music Man*. Most people left the show humming songs like "Seventy-Six Trombones" or "Goodnight, My Someone," but the song I remember the most is "(Ya Got) Trouble." River City's trouble was a pool hall, which many citizens felt would corrupt the young, but these days, the "pool hall" of our society is street violence, the angry rhetoric of politicians, and too many people who don't understand how government works.

Citizenship and government were key parts of the curriculum when I was in school. We learned that democracy means that the whole population contributes to government by electing officials to make laws and shape policies that best serve all citizens. It was drilled into our heads that the legislative, judicial, and executive branches of government have distinct purposes. We were taught that political parties have ideological differences and that it's important to know and understand how they differ as we determined our own political leaning. In those days, newspapers and the nightly news reported on prospective candidates for state and national offices, but there was no cable news "sensationalizing" the political process. I watched with great interest the night John F. Kennedy won the nomination for the Democratic Party in the summer of 1960. There had been some debate about his candidacy because of his religion, but it's likely it would have been a larger matter had there been 24/7 news coverage.

I know adults who aren't registered to vote, or who only vote the way their parents did. They are incapable of thinking critically about the real issues. It's quite possible that the reason for this apathy and lack of understanding about the political process is related to the K–12 curricula. The tenets of the Constitution are taught in U.S. history, but do we teach how this applies to the society in which we live? Is civics taught? Do students really understand the concept of voting? Are they given the opportunity to participate in decision-making that affects their lives in the classroom and total school environment? Do we give them the chance to debate topics in small groups and as a class? Are conclusions drawn when debate does occur?

There are a number of trade books that enlarge upon ideas and explanations presented in textbooks. Introduce the youngest students to books about the Constitution like *Shh! We're Writing the Constitution* (1987), by Jean Fritz and Tomie dePaola; *We the Kids: Preamble of the Constitution* (2002), by David Catrow; and *We the People* (1987), by Peter Spier.

Then give them *Amelia Bedelia's First Vote* (2012), by Herman Parish and

Lynne Avril; *Duck for President* (2004), by Doreen Cronin; *Grace for President* (2008), by Kelly Di Pucchio and LeUyen Pham; *Today on Election Day* (2012), by Catherine Stier and David Leonard; and *VOTE!* (2003), by Eileen Christelow. Have older readers take a look at *In Defense of Liberty: The Story of America's Bill of Rights* (2003), by Russell Freedman, and *A Kid's Guide to America's Bill of Rights* (rev. ed., 2015), by Kathleen Krull and Anna DiVito. Then suggest that they read *Presidential Elections and*

Other Cool Facts (2000), by Syl Sobel, and *Running for Office: A Look at Political Campaigns* (2003), by Sandy Donovan. Fiction that may help older readers understand the importance of elections includes *As If Being 12¾ Isn't Bad Enough, My Mother Is Running for President!* (2008), by Donna Gephart; *The Great Greene Heist* (2014), by Varian Johnson; *The Kid Who Ran for President* (2001), by Dan Gutman; and *Robert Takes a Stand* (2004), by Barbara Seuling.

Teaching the principles of good citizenship and offering books that explain our government and how it works are the only ways to avoid our version of "Trouble." It becomes the responsibility of schools and public libraries to influence the lives of the young by offering the information they need to make informed decisions when they reach voting age.

September 2016

PART 3

WHERE SCIENCE LEADS US

"We had prepared them so well for this day, yet we had not prepared them at all for what they saw."

THE MAN IN THE MOON

he Man in the Moon,

Looked out of the moon,

Looked out of the moon and said . . .

Now, if you are wondering what the Man in the Moon said, you are probably much younger than I. Just because I can complete this popular little ditty means only one thing: I grew up on nursery rhymes. That was the extent of my awareness of the heavenly bodies until I was much older. I think there was a chapter on the solar system in my seventh-grade science textbook, but I was never exposed to astronomy in high school until my senior year. That was the year that John Glenn orbited the earth. This event is etched in my memory not because of its historical significance, but for a very embarrassing reason.

The entire student body was hauled into the school auditorium to watch this important event. There were two small black-and-white televisions on the stage. Even those seated in the front row could barely see the tiny speck crossing the screen. That speck was *Friendship 7*, Glenn's space capsule. We sat there for the entire mission. It lasted 4 hours, 55 minutes, and a few seconds. But most of us missed it, and the commentary from NASA, because we were dodging spitballs or passing notes. We were simply bored. This is the embarrassing part.

There were two students who cared, and our bad behavior interfered with their desire to savor the moment. They were exchange students from Germany, and they didn't understand why American students were so apathetic and disrespectful. Our behavior was certainly inexcusable, but it wasn't totally our fault. Not one teacher had prepared us for this day. There was no lesson, no required reading, and no discussion at all. There wasn't even a follow-up lesson. We could have written about the event in English class, or we could have talked about the significance of this mission to the United States space program in government class. And "the sky's the limit" for what physics and math students could have discussed before and after Glenn's successful orbit.

We all have lessons learned from embarrassing moments. This column serves as a confession for what I have learned from mine. I never missed another spacecraft launch. I watched Neil Armstrong make his "giant leap for mankind." And when I became a middle-school librarian, I was determined to make my students care as my German classmates had cared. I

worked with the science teachers, and together we got students ready for each NASA event. They read, they wrote, and they were ready for each new space mission. We turned the library into a space research center. We talked with an astronaut by telephone. The students asked him what astronauts ate and how they slept in space. Of course, the most important question was how they dealt with bathroom needs.

In 1986, the entire sixth grade and their teachers gathered in the library to watch the *Challenger* liftoff. Unlike my high school, each classroom had a television, but the sixth-graders wanted to gather together to see it. They got very excited as they watched the seven *Challenger* crew members walk to the spacecraft. They were attentive as the liftoff occurred, and then, seconds later, they witnessed a disaster. We had prepared them so well for this day, yet we had not prepared them at all for what they saw. I know those students are now relating the events of that day to their own children. I hope they are also telling them about the many successful launches they witnessed, and how their teachers prepared them.

So, what did the Man in the Moon say? "Tis time that, now, I'm getting up, / All babies went to bed." I'm quite certain, though, that the successes of the NASA program would cause the Man in the Moon to issue a different decree today. I hope all the little ones are listening.

———— July 2009

Almost Astronauts: 12 Women Who Dared to Dream. By Tanya Lee Stone. 2009. 144p. Candlewick, $24.99 (9780763636111); paper, $17.99 (9780763645021).
These 13 women passed the physical tests to become astronauts, but then Vice President Lyndon B. Johnson told them that NASA wouldn't include women in the space program. This is their courageous fight to gain equality for women in a male-dominated field.

Astronauts. By Margaret J. Goldstein. 2017. 48p. Lerner, $31.99 (9781512425888).
The text, along with photographs and diagrams, answers questions about the challenges astronauts face and their contribution to research conducted on Earth. (Space Discovery Guides)

Liftoff: A Photobiography of John Glenn. By Don Mitchell. 2006. 64p. National Geographic, $29.90 (9780792259008).

John Glenn's career from fighter pilot in World War II to astronaut, and politician to the oldest man to fly in space is well documented with photos in this readable text.

Race to the Moon. By Steve Parker, Illus. by David West. 2015. 32p. Black Rabbit Books, $31.35 (97816258800789). Gr. 4–6.

This brief text traces the NASA programs from Mercury to *Explorer I*. (Story of Space Series).

MY MOTHER WAS
ROSIE THE RIVETER

y family has a scrapbook that chronicles my mother's life. In many ways, she was larger than life: she was a college graduate, but during WWII, she went to work at a shipyard in Mobile, Alabama, because they needed women to fill jobs vacated by men who were off fighting the war. My mother, who was five feet tall and weighed 98 pounds, worked a crane. Like Rosie the Riveter, she wore coveralls, rolled up her sleeves to reveal her muscles, and tied a scarf around her head to protect her hair from the machinery. When the men returned from war, most women returned to their places in the home and concentrated on growing their families. That never satisfied my mother. She performed the traditional women's roles during that time, but she also mowed the lawn, fixed the leaky faucets, repainted the house, laid tile in the kitchen, and built doll furniture for the girls in the family. She was excellent at math, and she could accurately calculate measurements, add columns of figures in her head, and predict the sum of the groceries in her shopping cart. Our family never took a trip without her recording the miles-per-gallon of gas we used in a notebook, kept in the glove compartment of the car. If she couldn't remember a specific statistic of the Atlanta Braves, she referred to a journal where she had it all written down.

My mother didn't talk that much about her "Rosie" years, but there are pictures in the scrapbook that document that time. She is now deceased, as are most women of her generation, but there are books for children that celebrate the important contribution that these women made to the war effort. *Rosie the Riveter: Women Working on the Home Front in World War II* (1998), by Penny Colman; *Slacks and Calluses: Our Summer in a Bomber Fac-*

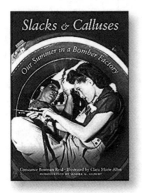

tory (2004), by Constance Bowman Reid and illustrated by Clara Marie Allen; and *American Women and World War II* (2009), by Doris Weatherford, should be available in libraries. Textbooks simply don't provide information about this period that trade books do.

Girls today are afforded more career opportunities than my mother's generation was, but a 2010 study conducted by the American Association of University Women reveals that there is still a gender gap in science, technology, and engineering. Schools across the nation are working to remedy this issue by offering more STEM-focused curricula. These programs encourage curiosity and imagination and help students develop skills necessary to compete in a global shift toward science and engineering fields.

Rosie the Riveter, and the women she represented, proved that a woman's role reaches far beyond the home. Girls must be led to understand that they have as much to offer as males, especially in careers traditionally held by men. Point to books that give them role models: *Fly High! The Story of Bessie Coleman* (2001), by Louise Borden and Mary Kay Kroeger; *Barbara McClintock: Genius of Genetics* (2006), by Naomi E. Pasachoff; *Marvelous Mattie: How Margaret E. Knight Became an Inventor* (2006), by Emily Arnold McCully; *Almost Astronauts: 13 Women Who Dared to Dream* (2009), by Tanya Lee Stone; *Silk and Venom: Searching for a Dangerous Spider* (2011), by Kathryn Lasky; *The Watcher: Jane Goodall's Life with the Chimps* (2011), by Jeanette Winter; *Look Up! Henrietta Leavitt, Pioneering Woman Astronomer* (2013), by

Robert Burleigh; and *Headstrong: 52 Women Who Changed Science—and the World* (2015), by Rachel Swaby.

My mother became a junior-high math teacher, but she never garnered a paycheck that was equal to her male colleagues; the justification for this was that "men were heads of households." Two of her granddaughters are university professors, and another is a midwife. One of the professors teaches architecture, and her male colleagues still enjoy slightly higher salaries. "You Can Do It" was Rosie the Riveter's slogan, and women like my mother proved they could. Now let's make sure today's girls realize they can, too.

— November 2016

Grace Hopper: Queen of Computer Code. By Laurie Wallmark. Illus. by Katy Wu. 2017. 48p. Stering, $16.95 (9781454920007).
This easy-to-read biography about a woman computer giant who was ahead of her time is an inspiration for young girls interested in science.

Margaret and the Moon: How Margaret Hamilton Saved the First Lunar Landing. By Dean Robbins. Illus. by Lucy Knisley. 2017. 32p. Knopf, $17.99 (9780399551857).
A pioneer in computer programming, Margaret Hamilton eventually achieved her greatest prominence when she landed a job at NASA and wrote codes for computer commands for the Apollo spacecraft missions.

Super Women: Six Scientists Who Changed the World. By Laurie Lawlor. 2017. 57p. Holiday House, $17.95 (9780823436750).
These six women, including Katherine Coleman Johnson, whose story was told in the movie *Hidden Figures*, faced discrimination in a white male-dominated field, and persevered to realize their dream of contributing to their chosen scientific field.

TALKING WITH
STEVE SHEINKIN

teve Sheinkin's *Bomb: The Race to Build—and Steal—the World's Most Dangerous Weapon* (2012) is an amazing account of the Manhattan Project. Its accolades are numerous: it was named a 2013 Newbery Honor Book, the 2013 Sibert Medal winner, and a 2012 National Book Award finalist. Skillfully merging science, history, and the personalities that made it all possible, this is one of the most comprehensive books for children on the topic. The well-documented text, filled with human-interest stories, and the numerous photographs lead young readers through an era of which they may know little about. What worried J. Robert Oppenheimer when the project was complete? The answer is what readers must ponder for their lives and future generations. In the conversation below, Sheinkin discusses the inspiration and research that went into *Bomb*, and he offers additional insights into writing informational books for youth.

SCALES: What inspired you to write about the Manhattan Project?
SHEINKIN: It was the spies that hooked me. I was fascinated by how the Soviets were able to steal bomb plans from this top-secret American lab. And

once I started reading about the subject, I couldn't stop.

SCALES: You provide an extended list of resources that support your research. How long did it take you to conduct the research? When did you realize that you had enough information to proceed with writing?

SHEINKIN: I spent about a year reading and taking notes. I'd still be doing research if I hadn't had a deadline to actually write something. I knew I had enough information to start writing, but I just enjoy the research process a lot more than the writing process.

SCALES: Did you uncover specific information in your research that surprised you?

SHEINKIN: Yes, some of the commando raids and secret-operations stories surprised me. I just didn't know these stories. My initial outline had nothing on the Norwegians parachuting behind enemy lines, but once I started learning about the story, I knew I had to put it in.

SCALES: You've written about Benedict Arnold and King George. How is writing about one historical character different from tackling the Manhattan Project, which included so many personalities?

SHEINKIN: I guess a story with fewer characters is a bit easier to organize. *Bomb* definitely felt like the most ambitious book I've tried, just because it had so much going on. So the challenge for me was structuring it very carefully, so that one story flowed into the next, hopefully without causing too much confusion.

SCALES: Who, other than Oppenheimer, did you find the most interesting?

SHEINKIN: There are too many to list, but the teenage physicist Theodore Hall was the first character to really grab me and pull me in. And, of course, everyone loves Richard Feynman. I had lots more on Feynman's antics with codes and safecracking at Los Alamos, but I had to cut it back just to keep things rolling.

SCALES: I recently met a woman who was a payroll clerk at Oak Ridge, Tennessee, in the 1940s. She has fond memories of the social life in the "secret town," although she had little awareness of what happened there beyond her job. Did you visit Los Alamos and Oak Ridge to get a sense of life in those places?

SHEINKIN: I visited Los Alamos, and I understood why [General Leslie] Groves and Oppenheimer liked the spot for a secret lab. I saw some of the old buildings, including the house on "Bathtub Row," where Oppenheimer lived, and lots of old pictures of daily life in the city. I'm fascinated by the stories of kids who lived at Los Alamos during the war—but that was another one of those subjects I just couldn't get into because of space!

SCALES: Oppenheimer had deep concerns about the atomic bomb after the war. In the epilogue, you challenge readers to think about the implications of the bomb on global warfare today. What do you hope readers will take away from this "warning"?

SHEINKIN: The main thing is just to be aware that these weapons are out there, and that we're going to have to decide what to do with them.

SCALES: Could you tell us about any memorable correspondence and feedback that you have received from young readers and teachers who have read your book?

SHEINKIN: Well, a few librarians have told me young readers have come into the library and asked where they can find plans for building an atomic bomb. That's not quite the reaction I was looking for, but at least they're engaged with the material!

SCALES: You are a former textbook writer. How do you compare writing nonfiction for young readers to writing content for textbooks?

SHEINKIN: Wow, there's no comparison. Writing for textbooks is about checking off a list of names, dates, topics—mentioned that, mentioned that, said that, now ask a review question. Writing narrative nonfiction is about telling stories. You're still trying to get across lots of information, but the goal is to do it through an entertaining narrative. I'm convinced the narrative approach is not only more fun for readers but more effective as well, since stories are much easier to remember than lists.

SCALES: Do you think that informational books for youth are evolving in response to the recently established awards focused just on nonfiction and with Common Core's emphasis on nonfiction in the classroom?

SHEINKIN: It may just be that more people are paying attention to the great nonfiction that's out there (check out the blog *Interesting Nonfiction for Kids*, where many of the best writers post: inkrethink.blogspot.com). The awards are a great incentive, but to be honest, I don't pay much attention to the Common Core stuff. I've read enough standards to last a lifetime. I just want to tell stories.

SCALES: What are you working on now?

SHEINKIN: I'm just finishing up a new book, set for publication in January 2014. It's called *The Port Chicago Fifty,* and it's a WWII civil rights story about a group of young African American sailors who stand up against segregation in the military. It's not a famous story at all, but it's very dramatic and, I think, an important one for people to know.

IN THE CLASSROOM

After students have read *Bomb,* have them read the mission of the Atomic Heritage Foundation. Lead a class discussion about the projects in which the foundation is currently involved. Then have them write a report that the director of the foundation presents to the board, aligning the foundation's projects with its mission statement. Encourage peer editing for clarity and grammar.

Ask students to listen to the stories of people who worked on the Manhattan Project. Why are oral histories so important? Instruct students to write a paragraph about each person that sums up his or her contribution to the project that might be included in the museum or library of the Manhattan Project National Historical Park.

Divide the class into small groups and ask them to study the Historical Walking Tour Map of Downtown Las Alamos. Then have them become tour guides for a walking tour of Los Alamos. Project the map on a screen, and ask each group to provide a narrative for their tour. Encourage them to provide a bibliography of books and websites they used in gathering information.

The novels and informational titles listed below will support student research and classroom units about the Manhattan Project.

FICTION

The Gadget. **By Paul Zindel. 2001. 192p. HarperCollins, $15.99 (9780060278120); paper, $6.99 (9780440229513).**
> In 1945, 13-year-old Stephen Orr joins his father, a physicist, in Los Alamos, New Mexico, and is unprepared to deal with the mystery of the top-secret world in which he must live.

The Green Glass Sea. **By Ellen Klages. 2006. 272p. Viking, $17.99 (9780670061341); paper, $8.99 (9780142411490).**
> It's 1943, and 10-year-old Dewey Kerrigan joins her father, a scientist, in Los Alamos. She knows very little about "the gadget" that occupies the time of the adults, but she finds the dump a perfect place to find parts for a radio that she is building.

The Year of the Bomb. **By Ronald Kidd. 2009. 208p. Simon & Schuster, $15.99 (9781416958925); paper, $5.99 (9781416996255).**
> Set in 1955 in a small California town, this novel's four seventh-grade boys investigate a professor from a nearby university who worked on the Manhattan Project.

NONFICTION

The Great Explainer: The Story of Richard Feynman. **By Harry LeVine. 2009. 144p. illus. Morgan Reynolds, lib. ed., $28.95 (9781599351131).**
> The personal story of Feynman, the man who was involved in building the atomic bomb, constructing the first computers, and figuring out why the

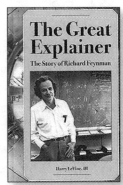

space shuttle *Challenger* exploded, appeals to young readers, even when the science may be too difficult for them.

J. Robert Oppenheimer: The Brain Behind the Bomb. By Glenn Scherer and Marty Fletcher. 2007. 128p. illus. Enslow, lib. ed., $33.27 (9781598450507).
This biography of the man who led the research at Los Alamos, the secret city where the atomic bomb was made, poses social and political questions about the ramifications of such a powerful war weapon, and the revelation that Oppenheimer had connections with the Communist Party.

The Manhattan Project. By Dan Elish. 2007. 48p. illus. Scholastic, $26 (9780516232997).
Documented with black-and-white photos of key scientists of the Manhattan Project, this book chronicles the scientific discoveries that led to America's development of nuclear weapons.

The Secret of the Manhattan Project. By Doreen Gonzales. 2012. 128p. illus. Enslow, $31.93 (9780766039544); paper, $9.95 (9781464400247).
Covering both history and science, this account of the development of the atomic bomb reveals the thousands of people in three top-secret towns it took to produce what became known as the Manhattan Project.

The Ultimate Weapon: The Race to Develop the Atomic Bomb. By Edward T. Sullivan. 2007. 192p. illus. Holiday, $24.95 (9780823418558).
Los Alamos, New Mexico, is considered the epicenter for the Manhattan Project, but this historical account introduces Oak Ridge, Tennessee, where enriched uranium was manufactured, and Hanford, Washington, where bomb-ready plutonium was developed.

SAMPLING SHEINKIN

Bomb: The Race to Build—and Steal—the World's Most Dangerous Weapon. By Steve Sheinkin. 2012. 272p. illus. Roaring Brook/Flash Point, $19.99 (9781596434875); e-book, $19.99 (9781596438613).

King George: What Was His Problem? By Steve Sheinkin. Illus. by Tim Robinson. 2008. 192p. Roaring Brook, $19.95 (9781596433199); paper, $8.99 (9781596435186); e-book, $8.99 (9781429931588).

Lincoln's Grave Robbers. By Steve Sheinkin. 2013. 224p. illus. Scholastic, $16.99 (9780545405720); e-book, $16.99 (9780545532266).

The Notorious Benedict Arnold: A True Story of Adventure, Heroism, & Treachery. By Steve Sheinkin. 2010. 352p. illus. Roaring Brook/Flash Point, $18.99 (9781596434868); paper, $8.99 (9781250024602); e-book, $9.99 (9781429951357).

Rabbi Harvey vs. the Wisdom Kid: A Graphic Novel of Dueling Jewish Folktales in the Wild West. By Steve Sheinkin. Illus. by the author. 2010. 144p. Jewish Lights, $16.99 (9781580234221).

Two Miserable Presidents: Everything Your Schoolbooks Didn't Tell You about the Civil War. By Steve Sheinkin. Illus. by Tim Robinson. 2008. 224p. Roaring Brook/Flash Point, $19.95 (9781596433205); paper, $9.99 (9781596435193); e-book, $9.99 (9781429932745).

—————————————————————————————— *September 2013*

Fallout. By Trudy Krisher. 2006. 272p. Holiday House, $17.95 (9780823420353).

It's 1954 and Genevieve's father, a faithful follower of Senator Joseph McCarthy, plans to build a fallout shelter in their backyard, but Genevieve begins to question her father's decision when she meets a new girl from California who has different political views.

Fallout. By Todd Strasser. 2013. 272p. Candlewick, $16.99 (9780763655341); paper, $8.99 (9780763876766).

Set during the Cuban Missile Crisis, Scott's father comes face-to-face with skeptical neighbors when he builds a fallout shelter in the backyard because he fears a nuclear war.

The Secret Project. By Jonah Winter. Illus. by Jeanette Winter. 2017. 32p. Simon & Schuster, $17.99 (9781481469135).

The scientists and other workers in the secret town of Los Alamos, New Mexico, live and work in complete isolation from the world as they develop the atom bomb, known to some as the "Gadget."

ARCHITECTURE
AND CONSTRUCTION

hildren have a natural interest in using blocks, Erector sets, Lincoln Logs, and LEGOs to build things. Sometimes they call upon their own creativity, and other times they follow detailed instructions that come with the construction set. This early introduction to building science often lays the groundwork for simple math and engineering skills.

Teachers can draw upon this natural interest as they plan a curriculum that applies math and science to the world around us. Perhaps students have seen photographs of some of the world's most iconic buildings, but they don't know how these buildings came to be. This annotated bibliography features nonfiction titles that focus on the ins and outs of building design and construction.

Architecture According to Pigeons. **By Speck Lee Tailfeather. Illus. by Natsko Seki. 2013. Phaidon, $19.95 (9789714863894).**

Pigeons, it turns out, are great admirers of attractive structures—it makes sense, doesn't it?—and one of the feathery fellows embarks on a tour of famous architectural wonders around the globe, which includes Fallingwater and Canterbury Cathedral.

Art and Architecture. **By Stephen M. Tomecek. 2010.**
  Facts on File, $35 (9781604131680).

> Twenty-five simple experiments to do in the
> classroom and at home help children under-
> stand the basic principles of architecture and
> mechanical arts by using common items like
> Magic Markers and toothpicks, and foods like
> blueberries and marshmallows.

Castle. **By David Macaulay. Illus. by the author.**
  1977 Houghton Mifflin Harcourt, $20
  (9780395257845).

> Detailed black-and-white sketches chronicle the building of a Welsh castle.
> Macaulay's trademark eye for detail turns this into a revelation of intricate
> whos, whats, and whys, with the whole thing ringing with wryness and
> humor.

Cathedral. **By David Macaulay. Illus. by the author. 1981. Houghton Mifflin Har-**
  court, $11.99 (9780395316689).

> This color version of the 1973 black-and-white classic reveals design
> details and construction techniques of the fictional Cathedral of Chutreaux.
> A Caldecott Honor Book, this takes a week-by-week approach, giving
> readers the chance to investigate every step and absorb its purpose.

The Golden Gate Bridge. **By Rebecca Stanborough.**
  2016. Capstone, $27.32 (9781491481967).

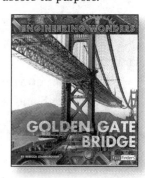

> Drawings and photographs, along with easy-
> to-read text, trace the engineering problems
> of building a bridge to withstand the "natural
> forces" of the San Francisco Bay. They were
> solved, though, and this book tells readers
> how.

The Hoover Dam. **By Jeffrey Zuehlke. 2009. Lerener,**
  $26.60 (9780822594086).

> Simple text relates this engineering spectacle and its purpose, though this
> entry into the Famous Places series draws much of its power from photos,
> both modern-day and period, the latter of which depict the seemingly
> death-defying efforts that went into construction.

If I Built a House. **By Chris Van Dusen. Illus. by the author. 2012. Penguin,**
  $16.99 (9780803737518).

> In this sequel to *If I Built a Car* (2005), Jack imagines a house of his
> dreams that includes a racetrack, a slide, and a room that flies. Long

rhymes with an inherently humorous bounce to them and Rube Gold-
bergesque illustrations make this a delight.

The LEGO Neighborhood Book. **By Brian Lyles and Jason Lyles. 2014. No
Starch, $19.95 (9781593275716).**
Who doesn't have a pile of these sitting around? The authors offer detailed
instructions to guide LEGO-lovers through the building of bases, basic
storefronts, and indoor and outdoor furniture. There are plenty of LEGO
books around, but this one is a keeper.

*Look at That Building: A First Book of
Structures*. **By Scot Ritchie. Illus. by
the author. 2011. Kids Can, $16.95
(9781554536962).**

A group of five children want to
build a doghouse, so they head to
the library for guidance. There they
learn about foundations, ceilings,
and design elements like domes and
columns. This book is smart, detailed,
yet conversational.

Maya Lin. **By Donald Langmead. 2011. Greenwood, $39 (9780313378539).**
Beginning with her life in China and her family's journey to relocate to the
United States, this solid book traces Lin's storied career as an architect,
with works including the Vietnam Veterans Memorial in Washington, DC.

Mr. Ferris and His Wheel. **By Kathryn Gibbs Davis. Illus. by Gilbert Ford. 2014.
HMH, $17.99 (9780547959221).**
Davis' suspense-filled prose and Ford's luminous illustrations fuel the story
of George Washington Gale Ferris Jr., inventor—under much duress—of
that engineering wonder the Ferris Wheel, which was finished in time for
the 1893 Chicago World's Fair.

Sky Boys: How They Built the Empire State Building. **By Deborah Hopkinson.
Illus. by James E. Ransome. 2006. Random/Schwartz & Wade, o.p.**
A second-person voice and free-verse style invite readers to participate in
the construction of the Empire State Building in Depression-era New York
City. The construction is documented with Ransome's bold illustrations,
while historic photographs of the building site accent the book's end pages.

Sky High. **By Germano Zullo. Illus. by Albertine. 2012. Chronicle, $18.95
(9781452113920).**
Witty and poetic, this book tells the story of a contest between two neighbors as they remodel, expand, and embellish their houses until they reach

skyscraper height. Fascinating, intricate line drawings slowly fill up the vertical trim size to wonderful effect.

Skyscraper. By Lynn Curlee. Illus. by the author. 2007. Atheneum, $19.99 (9780689844898).

In this overview of skyscrapers, Curlee moves from the first towering buildings, which rose in the aftermath of the Chicago fire, through the contemporary building scene and plans for the future. The clear, organized narrative and glowing acrylic portraits of skyscrapers both enthrall and educate.

There Goes the Neighborhood: 10 Buildings People Loved to Hate. By Susan Goldman Rubin. 2001. Holiday, $19.95 (9780823414352).

Rubin discusses the design and construction of such buildings as the Washington Monument, the Eiffel Tower, and the first McDonald's restaurant, all structures people hated as they were being erected, but over time grew to love.

This Bridge Will Not Be Gray. By Dave Eggers. Illus. by Tucker Nichols. 2015. McSweeney's, $19.95 (9781940450476).

This book focuses on the design elements of the Golden Gate Bridge, including how it came to be orange. An acclaimed author for adults, Eggers turns the true tale of architect Irving Morrow's bold idea into a quirky, whimsical, and enthusiastic crowd-pleaser.

The Three Little Pigs: An Architectural Tale. By Steven Guarnaccia. Illus. by the author. 2010. Abrams, $19.95 (9780810989412).

This fractured fairy tale has the three pigs playing the roles of famous architects Frank Gehry, Frank Lloyd Wright, and Philip Johnson as they construct highly designed houses in which to live. Surely one of them can withstand the wolf's huffing and puffing?

Who Built That? Skyscrapers: An Introduction to Skyscrapers and Their Architects. By Didier Cornille. Illus by author. 2014. Princeton Architectural, $16.95 (9781616892708).

Eight of the world's skyscrapers are presented with detailed information about the architects responsible for the vision, and the engineers in command of the construction. Cutaway illustrations of such structures as the Statue of Liberty will be revelations to young readers. Cornille also penned the companion title *Who Built That? Bridges* (2016).

Who Was Frank Lloyd Wright? **By Ellen Labrecque. Illus. by Gregory Copeland and Nancy Harrison. 2015. Grosset & Dunlap, $5.99 (9780448483139).**

>This biography of the "father of organic architecture" begins with his early life and covers some of his most iconic buildings like the Guggenheim Museum in New York City. The clear line drawings assist the straightforward chapter-book presentation.

Young Frank, Architect. **By Frank Viva. Illus. by the author. 2013. Abrams, $16.95 (9780870708930).**

>Frank Lloyd Wright lives with his grandfather, an architect who explains to his grandson that architecture is about designing buildings, not building things out of household items, as the boy is wont to do. The elder Frank takes his grandson to the Museum of Modern Art to inspire him—and readers.

IN THE CLASSROOM

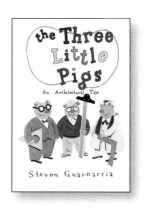

Read aloud *The Three Little Pigs: An Architectural Tale.* Then have students design a house for the pigs using items like rocks, paper, toilet paper, cardboard tubes, and LEGOs.

Use library books or websites to research the course of study for architecture and construction engineering. Then have students write a brief paper that discusses the skills it takes to enter one of these fields.

Have students read about a structure like the Eiffel Tower, the Vietnam Veterans Memorial, the Washington Monument, the entrance to the Louvre, the Guggenheim Museum, the National September 11 Memorial & Museum, or the USS Arizona Memorial at Pearl Harbor, and then write a front-page newspaper story on the day the structure was opened. Include pertinent information about the design and construction, and remember to include who, what, when, why, and how.

Break students into small groups and ask them to read about structures like the Hoover Dam or the Panama Canal. Then have them design a brochure that may be distributed to visitors of these engineering wonders.

Instruct them to locate pictures on the Internet to cut and paste into their brochure.

——————————————————————————————————— *November 2016*

Billions of Bricks. By Kurt Cyrus. 2016. 32p. Holt, $17.99 (9781627792738).
This counting book demonstrates all that is involved in constructing a building of brick.

Curious Constructions. By Michael Hearst. Illus. by Matt Johnston. 2017. 102p. Chronicle, $19.99 (9781452144849).
Bits of trivia, as well as scientific information, is provided on 50 structures, which includes the Nautilus House in Mexico City, Stonehenge in England, and the Great Wall of China.

Maya Lin: Artist-Architect of Light and Lines: Designer of the Vietnam Veterans Memorial. By Jeanne Walker Harvey. Illus. by Dow Phumiruk. 2017. 32p. Holt, $17.99 (9781250112491).
This picture-book biography begins with Lin's childhood and continues through the design and completion of the Vietnam Veterans Memorial in Washington DC.

ON THE STREET
WHERE I LIVED

here were a number of kids on my street when I was growing up, and we spent a lot of time together. We played pickup games of softball, raced go-carts down a steep hill in front of my house, and built hideouts in a nearby wooded area. We shared library books, ghost stories, and our love of *I Love Lucy* or *The Roy Rogers Show*. I thought I knew all the kids and their families well, but I was in college before I learned why the two sisters who lived at the end of my street sat on their front steps crying as they watched a car pull away with their mother in the passenger seat. It turns out that their mother suffered from mental illness and was committed to the state mental hospital for months at a time.

In another house, just behind us, a girl my sister's age lived with her paternal grandparents. Her father was sometimes there, but I never heard anyone mention her mother until the day I overheard two women on my street whispering that Mrs. Jones was in a tuberculosis sanatorium. I had never heard of tuberculosis, and to this day, I don't understand why they felt the need to whisper.

My best friend lived next door. She was an only child, and we were inseparable until we got to high school. I was in her home a lot, and I have a vague memory of seeing her dad occasionally stagger in at night and her mother pace up and down the driveway wringing her hands. Not a word was spoken about what was going on in that home. Then, when I was much older, I understood that the mother's nervous condition was caused by the dad's problem with alcohol. He outlived her.

When I was in kindergarten, a girl with polio moved just a few houses down the street. We all wanted crutches like hers until we visited her when she was hospitalized at Warm Springs, the hospital in Georgia that Franklin D. Roosevelt made famous. Seeing kids in iron lungs and in wheelchairs or on gurneys with both legs paralyzed changed our wish, and not one of us protested when the county health department came to our school to administer the polio vaccine.

None of the books in our school library offered even a glimpse into the lives of families like the ones on my street. There was Colin, the handicapped boy in Frances Hodgson Burnett's *The Secret Garden*. But no character had a father who drank too much, or a mother who suffered from mental illness. There were characters who died of smallpox, yellow fever, diphtheria, and various plagues in historical fiction, but these devastating epidemics were often incidental to the plot of the stories.

How much more informed we would have been about public health issues if we had had books like *Fever, 1793,* by Laurie Halse Anderson; and *The Great Trouble: A Mystery of London, the Blue Death, and a Boy Called Eel,* by

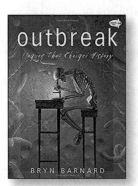

Deborah Hopkinson. I'm certain that science and social studies classes would have been more interesting and memorable if there had been books like *Outbreak! Plagues That Changed History,* by Bryn Barnard; *An American Plague: The True and Terrifying Story of the Yellow Fever Epidemic of 1793,* by Jim Murphy; and *The Purple Death: The Mysterious Flu of 1918,* by D. Getz.

Immunizations were required but never explained to us. We all wailed when the county nurse lined us up for a yearly typhoid shot, but we may have quieted if we had read *Letters from Rifka,* by Karen Hess. The necessity of the smallpox vaccination would have been evident if *A House of Tailors,* by Patricia Reilly Giff, had been available to us.

Children may be more aware of the realities of devastating illnesses today. But a little knowledge doesn't build empathy in the same way a story does. I'm certain I would have shown compassion for some of the kids on the street where I lived if there had been books like *Nest,* by Esther Ehrlich, about a girl whose mother suffers a mental illness, or *Breathing Room,* by Marsha Hayles, which tells the story of a girl who is hospitalized with tuberculosis. Even though polio was very real to me, I know I would have read *Chasing Orion,* by Kathryn Lasky, because it is about a new girl in the neighborhood who has polio. Give children stories, and they will become kinder and gentler toward those who are suffering, whether it's on the street where they live or in another part of the nation or world.

November 2014

Auma's Long Run. **By Eucabeth A. Odhi-ambo. 2017. 304p. Lerner, $17.99 (9781512427844). Gr. 3–6.**
Set in Kenya, Auma has dreams of attending high school and eventually becoming a doctor, but when the AIDS epidemic hits her small village she must decide whether to chase her dream or stay behind and help her family and village.

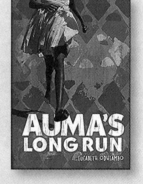

Terrible Typhoid Mary. **By Susan Campbell Bartoletti. 2015. 240p. Houghton Mifflin Harcourt, $17.99 (9780544313675). Gr. 7-up.**
Mary Mallon, an Irish immigrant, was the suspected carrier of typhoid fever in the early 1900s, was tried as a menace to society, and lived most of her life in quarantine.

FAMILIES COPING
WITH MENTAL ILLNESS

isa, *Bright and Dark,* by John Neufeld, was published in 1969 and was considered a groundbreaking book because it portrayed a teenager suffering from mental illness. At the time, adults had a tough time dealing with this book because they felt it was too dark for young minds. Yet the National

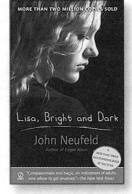

Alliance on Mental Illness says that 1 in 5 adults suffer some type of mental illness, and 1 in 5 youth ages 13 to 18 experience severe mental illness. The figures are slightly lower for younger children. Mental illness is a science issue, but it is also a social one. Schools deal with problems related to mental illness on a daily basis. Sometimes it's a child who suffers a mental disorder, but it's often a child who lives within a family plagued by mental illness.

There's recently been a groundswell of books dealing with the latter, featuring young protagonists faced with parents or siblings struggling with mental health issues. Susan Vaught's recent novel, *Footer Davis Probably Is Crazy* (2015), follows sixth-grader Footer as things around her spiral out of control. Her mother, who suffers from bipolar disorder, quits taking her medicine and is committed to a mental hospital. Nine days earlier, someone shot her neighbor Mr. Abrams and burned his farm to the ground. Cissy and Doc, two children who had been left in the care of their now-dead grandfather, haven't been seen since that tragic night. Footer and her best friend, Peavine Jones, are determined to solve the mystery, but Footer's father, a local policeman, doesn't want the kids poking around the site  of the crime. The problem is that Footer has memories of the night of the fire—thoughts that she was actually there and that maybe her mother was involved. She tells her father about her memories, but he won't listen.

Footer misses her mother so much that she enters her parents' bedroom in hopes that her mother's smells will make her feel present. She spots a stationery box on her mother's desk and finds letters between her mother and Carl Abrams, Cissy and Doc's father, who is in prison. Then there is a phone call for her mother from a woman who says, "Look, you tell your mama I can't do it. Get that?" This, of course, further raises Footer's suspicion that her mother was involved with the fire. Footer is so disturbed by her discovery that she records her thoughts in a notebook.

When her mother seems well enough to see her, Footer's father takes her to the hospital and allows mother and daughter a little time alone. Footer gains the courage to ask about the fire, and her mother becomes so agitated that the nurses must calm her down. Back home, a series of other events causes her dad to confess, "I'm afraid of losing your mother, just like you are. I'm afraid of losing you—my family, everything I love." Footer asks if he thinks she is crazy like her mother. He replies, "I think you're perfect and smart and pretty and strong, and nothing else matters. Whatever comes down the road later, we'll deal with it."

Footer's struggle to not only manage her feelings about her ailing mother but also her growing worry that she might be headed down the same path is one that might resonate for many young readers. The following list of titles address this issue and others.

FICTION

Afternoon of the Elves. By Janet Taylor Lisle. 1999. Open Road, e-book, $3.99 ((9781453297124).

Sara-Kate builds a tiny village in her overgrown backyard for the elves and shares it with nine-year-old Hillary. The two become friends until Sara-Kate is sent to live with relatives when her mentally ill mother is institutionalized.

Chasing the Milky Way. By Erin E. Moulton. 2014. Philomel, $16.99 (9780399164491).

Twelve-year-old Lucy Peevey has plans for a better life away from the Sunnyside Trailer Park, where she lives with her single mother and little sister, but things go awry when her mother's bipolar disorder spirals out of control.

Crazy. By Han Nolan. 2012. Houghton, $8.99 (9780547577289).

Fifteen-year-old Jason is left to care for his mentally ill father after his mother dies of a stroke. Various social service agencies help Jason cope and learn to deal with the haunting worry that he might have inherited his father's illness.

A Finders-Keepers Place. By Ann Haywood Leal. 2010. Holt, $7.99 (9781429962018).

Set in the 1970s, 11-year-old Esther tries to hold her poverty-ridden family together after their father leaves home and her mentally ill mother spends days in bed.

Footer Davis Probably Is Crazy. By Susan Vaught. 2015. Simon & Schuster, $16.99 (9781481422765).

Footer Davis is in the sixth grade when her mother is hospitalized after she quits taking her medicine for bipolar disorder. Faint memories of a tragic fire cause Footer to wonder if she is "crazy" like her mother.

Getting Near to Baby. By Audrey Couloumbis. 1999. Penguin, $6.99 (9780698118928).

Thirteen-year-old Willa Jo and her little sister are spending time with Aunt Patty and Uncle Hob because their mother is suffering a severe mental depression after the death of their baby sister.

Humming Whispers. By Angela Johnson. 1995. Scholastic, o.p.

Fourteen-year-old Sophy is worried that she may suffer from schizophrenia like her older sister, and she finds support from her friends and Aunt Shirley, her surrogate mother.

Nest. **By Esther Ehrlich. 2014. Random/Wendy Lamb, $16.99 (9780385386074).**

Naomi "Chirp" Orenstein is 11 the year her mother, a dancer, is hospitalized for mental depression, and she struggles as her father, a psychiatrist, tries to hold the family together when their lives appear to be unraveling.

Rabble Starkey. **By Lois Lowry. 1987. HMH, e-book, $17 (9780547345390).**

Rabble's mother, Sweet Hosanna, works for the Bigelows, and when Mrs. Bigelow is committed to a mental institution after she tries to drown her young son, Sweet Hosanna and Mr. Bigelow begin a romance.

Rocky Road. **By Rose Kent. 2010. Knopf, $7.99 (9780375863455).**

Twelve-year-old Tess Dobson's mother suffers from bipolar disorder, and in one of her manic moments, she decides to move the family from Texas to Schenectady, New York, and open an ice cream store.

Silhouetted by the Blue. **By Traci L. Jones. 2011. Farrar, $16.99 (9780374369149).**

Serena is in the seventh grade when she must take over the household because of her father's debilitating depression after her mother dies.

Small as an Elephant. **By Jennifer Richard Jacobson. 2011. Candlewick, $15.99 (9780763641559).**

Eleven-year-old Jack struggles to survive after his mentally ill mother abandons him at a campground in Maine.

So B. It. **By Sarah Weeks. 2004. Harper, $16.99 (9780066236223).**

Heidi is 12 years old when she decides to search for details of her background and the cause of her mother's mental disorder.

Sure Signs of Crazy. **By Karen Harrington. 2013. Little, Brown, $17 (9780316210584).**

Seventh-grader Sarah Nelson looks for signs that she may be "crazy" like her mother, who was institutionalized after she tried to drown her twins 10 years earlier.

The Whole Story of Half a Girl. **By Veera Hiranandani. 2013. Yearling, $6.99 (9780375871672).**

Sonia Nadhamuni is in the sixth grade when her dad loses his job and causes a financial crisis for the family. She has to leave private school and go to a public middle school where she knows no one. To make matters worse, her dad is suffering from a severe clinical depression.

SERIES NONFICTION

Encyclopedia of Psychological Disorders (series). Chelsea House.
Mental Illness and Its Effect on School and Work Environments. By Charles J.
   Shields. 2000. illus. o.p.

Essential Issues (series). ABDO
Mental Disorders. By Courtney Farrell. 2010. illus. $35.64 (9781604539561).

Inside Science (series). ReferencePoint.
Mental Illness Research. By Carla Mooney. 2011. illus. $37.27 (9781601522344).

The State of Mental Illness and Its Therapy (series). Mason Crest.
The FDA and Psychiatric Drugs. By Joan Esherick. 2013. illus. $24.95
   (9781422228265).
Mood Disorders. By Joan Esherick. 2013. illus. $24.95 (9781422228296).
   • *Psychosomatic Disorders*. By Autumn Libal. 2013. illus. $24.95
      (9781422228340).
   • *Schizophrenia*. By Shirley Brinkerhoff. 2013. illus. $24.95
      (9781422228357).

Understanding Mental Disorders (series). ReferencePoint.
What Is Anxiety Disorder? By Carla Mooney. 2015. illus. $28.95
   (9781601529206).
What Is Bipolar Disorder? By Andrea Nakaya. 2015. illus. $28.95
   (9781601529220).
What Is Panic Disorder? By Carla Mooney. 2015. illus. $28.95 (9781601529244).
What Is Schizophrenia? By Melissa Abramovitz. 2015. illus. $28.95
   (9781601529268).

USA Today Health Reports: Diseases and Disorders (series). Lerner.
Depression. By Wendy Moragne. 2011. illus. $34.60 (9780761358824).

What's the Issue? (series). Compass Point.
More Than the Blues: Understanding Depression. By Carla Mooney. 2009. illus.
   $27.99 (9780756542658).

The following are suggestions for exploring mental illness among family
members with a focus on Susan Vaught's *Footer Davis Probably Is Crazy*.

BOOK DISCUSSION

   • Cite scenes from the novel that reveal that Footer's mother is a
      good mom when she is mentally healthy.

- Footer says that her mother got "different" sometimes. Discuss the times that her mother's behavior is "different" or abnormal. How does this affect the entire family?
- Trace Footer's relationship with her dad from the beginning of the novel to the end. Why doesn't he listen to Footer when she tries to tell him what she remembers from the night of the fire?
- Stephanie Bridges, an employee of the Mississippi Department of Human Services' Family and Children's Services, comes to school to talk with Footer after her mother goes to the hospital. How is the social worker an advocate for Footer? At the end of the novel, Footer refers to Stephanie as her friend. What causes her to change her attitude toward Stephanie?
- Describe the friendship between Footer and Peavine. Why are Footer and Peavine so interested in the mystery surrounding the fire at the Abrams' farm? What do they discover?
- Explain why Footer keeps a "Really Probably Crazy List." How does her dad reassure her that she is not "crazy"?
- Footer and her dad go to the hospital to see her mother. Why does bringing up the fire at the Abrams' farm upset her mother? How does her mother's reaction make Footer feel guilty? Discuss what her dad means when he says, "Your mom isn't anybody's fault" (p.186).

FURTHER EXPLORATION OF MENTAL ILLNESS

- Footer's mother suffers from bipolar disorder. Read about bipolar disorder on the following website: http://bit.ly/1LVxXXY. Then ask students to write a notebook entry that draws a parallel between Footer's mother's behaviors and those outlined on the website.
- There are people who are very supportive of Footer when her mother is in the hospital. Jot down all the ways the following characters help Footer: Captain Armstrong, Ms. Malone, Stephanie Bridges, and Mrs. Jones. Then have students write a thank-you letter that Footer might write to one of them.
- Research an organization in the community that helps families affected by mental illness. It may be a local chapter of NAMI, the

Department of Family and Children's Services, or the local hospital. Then have students develop a brochure that outlines the purpose and services of one of the organizations.

November 2015

Get Well Soon. **By Julie Halpern. 2009. 224p. Macmillan paper, $9.99 (9780312581480). Gr. 7-up.**
Anna Bloom is committed to a mental hospital after she suffers a series of panic attacks and severe depression.

Lily and Dunkin. **By Donna Gephart. 2016. 352p. Delacorte, $16.99 (9780553536744). Gr. 5-up.**
None of the eighth graders know that Lily is transgender and Dunkin suffers from bipolar disorder, but as the story develops the two become friends and slowly reveal the secrets they have been harboring.

PART 4

WHEN ART INSPIRES US

"He could draw and he was good. He made small sketches in the margins of his school notebooks and made larger drawings on the unused sides of scrap paper that he took from the wastebasket."

A LESSON
FROM FRANK

**first met Frank when he was in the seventh grade. It** was the middle of the year when he enrolled in the school where I served as librarian. He came into the library and requested a library card and asked about library rules. He seemed surprised when I told him the rules: (1) come to the library as often as you like; (2) borrow as many books as you want; (3) keep the books as long as you need them; and (4) no overdue fines. Frank looked stunned and said, "I like these rules. That's not like my old school."

This wasn't the only time that Frank referred to his "old school." It happened again as he discovered the library's collection. One day he said to me, "This library has books that I'm interested in. My old school just had black history books." I told Frank that we celebrated black history in our school too, and that we had plenty of books with African American main characters, and nonfiction works to celebrate and teach the tremendous contributions of African Americans in our society. He responded by saying, "I know, but that's not all you have."

Though Frank cared a lot about his African American heritage, he also had a passion for art. He didn't know anything about art styles or the various art mediums. He couldn't name a single artist. He could draw and he was good. He made small sketches in the margins of his school notebooks and made larger drawings on the unused sides of scrap paper that he took from the wastebasket. Frank pored over the art books that he discovered in the library of his "new school." He was happy to learn that Horace Pippin and Jacob Lawrence were famous African American artists, but he was equally happy to discover Klee, Picasso, Matisse, Monet, and Pollock.

One day I asked Frank to tell me about his "old school." He had attended an inner-city school in a very large city in the Northeast. The student population was predominately African American. The primary focus of the school was on keeping order; therefore, the students had little opportunity to explore personal interests. They could only go to the library as a class, and the library was closed after school. Frank informed me that the only time his class went to the library was to "do reports on black history." It's possible that Frank's "old school" did have books in the collection about subjects other than black history. Maybe his perception of the library was shaped by the assignments that he had been given. Could it be that the teachers in Frank's "old school" made the false assumption that African American students only want to read about African Americans? If Frank was correct and the library only had books about black history, then the librarian was misguided as well. The students in Frank's "new school," regardless of ethnicity, enjoyed the works of Christopher Paul Curtis, Sharon M. Draper, Virginia Hamilton, Angela Johnson, Patricia C. and Fredrick L. McKissack, Walter Dean Myers, Marilyn Nelson, Mildred D. Taylor, and Jacqueline Woodson. And students in his "new school" were interested in learning about Charles Drew, Gordon Parks, Jesse Owens, Rosa Parks, Shirley Chisholm, Barbara Jordan, Louis Armstrong, and of course, Martin Luther King Jr. They were interested because the teachers helped them understand how people of all cultures and races have shaped this nation and will help mold its future.

As we celebrate Black History Month this year, I hope that every librarian and teacher will learn a lesson from Frank. African American students want to know about the heroes and heroines of their own race. They want to read works of fiction that reflect their own lives. But that isn't all they want. They want to have access to books and materials that allow them the chance to explore their own personal interests. For Frank, that interest was art. I hope that he has become a successful artist. If not, I'm quite certain that he could teach collection development in a library school.

January 2009

A Splash of Red: The Life and Art of Horace Pippin. **By Jen Bryant. Illus. by Melissa Sweet. 2013. 40p. Knopf, $17.99 (9780375867125).**

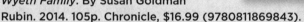

This simple text tells the life of a self-taught artist who managed to overcome poverty and racism and become a household name among American art enthusiasts.

Everyone Paints! The Lives and Art of the Wyeth Family. **By Susan Goldman Rubin. 2014. 105p. Chronicle, $16.99 (9780811869843).**

The lives and works of three generations of the Wyeth dynasty are revealed, including their troubled family dynamics. Color reproductions of all three artists are included.

George Bellows: Painter with a Punch. **By Robert Burleigh. 2012. 40p. Abrams, $19.95 (9781419701665).**

This short biography of the artist known for portraying the busy streets of New York City and ringside views of boxing matches includes boyhood photographs and reproductions of his art.

Jacob Lawrence: A Painter's Story. **By Sneed B. Collard III. 2009. 48p. Marshall Cavendish, $29.93 (9780761440581).**

Lawrence's life in Harlem, his work with the WPA, and his World War II service are discussed, but the focus is on his art. There are alternating pages of text and reproductions of his art, as well as period photographs. (American Heroes Series)

Keith Haring: The Boy Who Just Kept Drawing. **By Kay A. Haring. Illus. by Robert Neubecker. 2017. 32p. Dial, $16.99 (9780525428190).**

This picture-book biography of the famous American Pop artist reveals his early passion for art and how he developed a love and interest in street art.

E. L. KONIGSBURG'S
THE SECOND
MRS. GIACONDA

AN UPDATE

y "Book Strategies" column for the first issue of *Book Links* (November 15, 1990) featured *The Second Mrs. Giaconda,* E. L. Konigsburg's story about Leonardo da Vinci and the painting of the *Mona Lisa.* This novel has been successfully presented to sixth-grade students in my school for a number of years, and is appropriate for older readers as well; furthermore, it clearly links art, history, science, and literature. For this reason, we feel that it is fitting to celebrate five years of *Book Links* by updating the article on Konigsburg's extraordinary work of literature.

Konigsburg presents Leonardo as a gifted artist, scientist, and student who was so "concerned about the future that he couldn't relax in the now." He seldom finished projects and therefore was not credited with some of his most brilliant accomplishments. The novel, set in Milan, Italy, in the six-teenth century at the height of the High Renaissance, finds Leonardo much in demand as an artist. Dukes, duchesses, kings, and queens beg him to paint their portraits, but Leonardo is bored with the "noble types" and elects to paint less important subjects.

In the opening chapter, Leonardo catches a young thief, Salai, in the act of picking a pocket and, intrigued by the boy's attitude toward life, offers the rascal an apprenticeship. "Having for a brief moment thought that God had him by the back of his hair, it was something of a disappointment to learn that it was only Leonardo da Vinci." The scene establishes Konigsburg's thesis: that the untamed energy of Salai was crucial to Leonardo's success as an artist. Although Salai continually steals Leonardo's art sketches and sells them, Leonardo keeps him on as his assistant and even remembers him in his will. Ultimately, Salai leads his master to the subject that becomes his most famous painting of all—the *Mona Lisa.*

Konigsburg relies on research to support her theory that the subject of the *Mona Lisa* was indeed the wife of a common merchant. The author clearly and accurately describes life during the Renaissance and introduces readers to a number of sixteenth-century personalities. Scenes revolve around the marriage of Duke Ludovico Sforza of Milan (Leonardo's patron) and the rather plain but fabulously interesting Beatrice; the duke's infidelities and Beatrice's attempts at gaining his love; and Beatrice's jealous sister Isabella's unsuccessful attempts at getting Leonardo to paint her portrait. The book, written in the third person, uses witty dialogue to reveal character. The vocabulary is challenging, and the opportunities for research are numerous.

For students to enjoy studying this period in history and to realize the full value of the novel's literary contribution—middle and junior high curricula are often deficient in Renaissance studies—*The Second Mrs. Giaconda* must be carefully presented.

SETTING THE SCENE

- Exhibit art prints by Leonardo and other Renaissance artists, such as Michelangelo and Raphael. Be sure to include the following prints, all of which are mentioned in the novel: a Leonardo self-portrait, the *Mona Lisa*, and Leonardo's portrait of Cecilia Gallerani.
- Search your school and public library for art books or even more general titles dealing with the Renaissance.

- Display full-color photographs or large posters or show slides of Florence and Milan, where much of the story takes place.
- Introduce the novel by sharing biographical material on Konigsburg, making specific references to her love of art.

RESEARCH

- Suggest that students research biographical information about Leonardo and present it to the class.
- Some students might research the culture and daily life of the Florentines and Milanese, identifying the major artists and artworks that characterize the period, and share their findings.
- Divide students into small groups, asking each to prepare and present a short biographical sketch (including artistic works) of one of the major Renaissance artists.
- Students might develop a one-page character sketch of Beatrice, or any other major character in the novel.
- Have students choose and research one of the following topics: the daily life of the rich and the poor of the Renaissance; the state of science and medicine during the Renaissance; why the *Mona Lisa*, painted by an Italian, is hanging in the Louvre in Paris, France; and why religion played such an important role in the paintings of the Renaissance. While preparing the reports, students might underline new words used in their writing and then include a glossary defining these words at the end of the report. At least three sources should be used, and proper bibliographic information cited.

DISCUSSION

- What does Konigsburg mean when she says, "Salai was chosen [as Leonardo's apprentice] because he was sensitive—which made him a good audience—and not serious—which made him no threat"?
- What are some of the jobs that Salai had to do as Leonardo's apprentice?
- Why was Beatrice referred to as a "woman of layers"?
- How is Leonardo's study of anatomy and botany revealed in his paintings?
- Describe Leonardo's relationship with Michelangelo.

BIBLIOGRAPHY

Arenas, Jose Fernandez. *The Key to Renaissance Art*. 1990. 80p. Lerner, $16.13 (0822520575).

>Arenas deftly puts the Renaissance into context for young readers as he describes the history and main characteristics of the period and examines paintings (including Leonardo's *Adoration of the Magi*), architecture, and sculpture.

Bender, Michael. *Waiting for Filippo: The Life of Renaissance Architect Filippo Brunelleschi*. 1995. 10p. Chronicle, $19.95 (0811801810).

>This intricate pop-up book reveals some of the splendid buildings constructed during the Renaissance and gives an introduction to the man who built them.

Corsi, Jerome R. *Leonardo da Vinci: A Three-Dimensional Study*. 1995. 12p. Pomegranate, Box 6099, Rohnert Park, CA 94927, $19.95 (1566409888).

>Six double-page images reveal, in three-dimensional format, Leonardo's genius. His proportions for the human figure, his concept of a flying machine, and his painting of *The Last Supper* are included.

Cumming, Robert. *Just Imagine: Ideas in Painting*. 1982. 64p. Scribner. o.p.

>Colorful reproductions of well-known artworks guide young people toward developing a sense of the intellectual and emotional content of a painting.

Davidson, Rosemary. *Take a Look: An Introduction to the Experience of Art*. 1994. 128p. Viking, $18.99 (0670844780).

>A history of art, as well as a discussion of the techniques and functions of art, is presented through a variety of paintings, representing many different cultures. Also note H. W. and Anthony F. Janson's *The History of Art for Young People* (Abrams).

Horris, Nathaniel. *Leonardo and the Renaissance*. 1987. 48p. Bookwright, o.p.

>After an opening chapter on the master painter, the author looks at the Renaissance, including the culture, the lifestyles of the people, and the spread of the movement across Europe.

Hurd, Thatcher. *Art Dog*. 1996. 32p. HarperCollins, $14.95 (0060244240).

>For a bit of whimsy, read aloud this amusing picture book in which Mona Woofa plays a pivotal role.

Kettelkamp, Larry. *Computer Graphics: How It Works, What It Does*. 1989. 144p. Morrow, $12.95 (0688075045).

In a section called "Computer Graphics at Work," Kettelkamp describes how a specialist at Bell Laboratories in New Jersey used computer graphics to support a theory that the *Mona Lisa* is actually a self-portrait of Leonardo. Readers will be fascinated by this idea, contrasted with Konigburg's theory about the subject of the famous painting.

Lafferty, Peter. *Leonardo da Vinci.* 1990. 48p. Bookwright, o.p.

Lafferty emphasizes Leonardo's research and inventions in this introductory discussion about his life.

L'Engle, Madeleine. *The Glorious Impossible.* 1990. 64p. Simon & Schuster, $19.95 (0671686909).

Reproductions of Giotto's frescoes from the Scrovegni Chapel in Padua, Italy, grace these pages in beautiful full color, offering an excellent detailed picture of frescoes—an art form that Leonardo worked in and that is referred to in Konigsburg's novel.

Marshall, Norman V. *Leonardo da Vinci.* Illus. by Aldo Ripamonti. 1990.112p. Silver Burdett, $16.98 (0382099826); paper, $8.95 (0382240073).

In this profile, several paragraphs address Marshall's interpretation of the story behind the *Mona Lisa*. An appended chronology and a note on Leonardo's observations of nature will be helpful for student research.

Mason, Antony. *Leonardo da Vinci.* 1994. 32p. Barron's, $10.95 (0812064607); paper, $5.95 (0812019970).

This picture-book biography introduces the painter and his works.

McLanathan, Richard. *Leonardo da Vinci.* 1990. 96p. Abrams, $17.95 (0810912562).

This elegantly presented overview of Leonardo explores the man's life and paintings and his ideas about science, nature, music, and machines.

Meltzer, Milton. *Columbus and the World Around Him.* 1990. 288p. Watts, $15.40 (0531108996).

Columbus was a contemporary of Leonardo; in this book, Meltzer illuminates the world that the two men, unknown to each other, lived in.

Morrison, Taylor. *Antonio's Apprenticeship: Painting a Fresco in Renaissance Italy.* 1996. 32p. Holiday, $15.95 (082341213X).

Antonio, an apprentice in his uncle's, paint shop, relates his work on a series of frescoes for a chapel in Florence. Morrison's images reveal the time as well as the needed skills of the artists.

Muhlberger, Richard. *What Makes a Leonardo a Leonardo?* 1994. 48p. Viking, paper, $11.99 (0670857440).

A discussion of Leonardo's art, with both partial and complete reproductions of several of his paintings, provides insights into the man's genius.

Osman, Karen. *The Italian Renaissance.* 1996. 112p. Lucent, $16.95 (1560062371).

Osman examines the history, achievements, and legacy of the Renaissance in Italy, giving emphasis to Florence and Rome.

Pekarik, Andrew. *Painting: Behind the Scenes.* 1992. 60p. Hyperion, $18.95 (1562822969).

While there is no reference to Leonardo in this book, numerous reproductions and discussions of famous paintings help readers understand how to look at art.

Provenson, Alice, and Martin Provenson. *Leonardo da Vinci: The Artist, Inventor, Scientist in Three-Dimensional Movable Pictures.* 1984. 12p. Viking, $17.95 (067042384X).

Six well-engineered spreads depict such Florentine scenes as Leonardo's apprentice trying out a flying machine, the painter and his students at work, and the master observing the night sky in the shadow of a three-dimensional astrolabe.

Raboff, Ernest. *Leonardo da Vinci.* 1987. 32p. HarperCollins, o.p.

Reproductions of Leonardo's masterpieces as well as cartoons or sketches of his work give focus to the simple text.

Romei, Francesca. *Leonardo do Vinci: Artist, Inventor and Scientist of the Renaissance.* Illus. by Sergio and Andrea Ricciardi. 1995. 64p. Peter Bedrick, $19.95 (0872263134).

The use of an oversize format provides space for large, clear reproductions as well as captioned drawings and informative text.

Skira-Venturi, Rosabianca. *A Weekend with Leonardo da Vinci.* 1993. 64p. Rizzoli, $19.95 (0847814408).

Written as though the reader is being invited to share a weekend with Leonardo, this book provides insights into the artist's life, but, unfortunately, not into the identity of the subject of the *Mona Lisa.*

Ventura, Piero. *Great Painters.* 1984. 160p. Putnam, o.p.

The chronological order of this discussion of great painters from Giotto to Picasso places Leonardo and his contemporaries in context for young researchers.

Waters, Elizabeth, and Annie Harris. *Painting: A Young Artist's Guide.* 1993. 48p. DK, $14.95 (1564583481).

Using references to famous works of art, this book introduces young artists to various techniques of painting.

Wood, Tim. *The Renaissance*. 1993. 48p. Viking, $14.99 (0670851493).

> See-through pages and reproductions of numerous artworks invite readers to explore the life and culture of the Renaissance.

Woolf, Felicity. *Picture This: A First Introduction to Painting*. 1990. 40p. Doubleday, $14.95 (0385411359).

> This introduction provides a two-page spread on frescoes as an art form.

———————————————————————— *March 1996*

Leonardo Da Vinci. By Kathleen Tracy. 2008. 48p. Mitchell Lane, $29.95 (9781584157113).

> This brief book chronicles the life and works of the artist. (Art Profiles for Kids Series)

Leonardo da Vinci and the Renaissance in World History. By Allison Lassieur. 2000. 120p. Enslow, $19.95 (9780766014015).

> Readers are presented with a broad view of the Renaissance and how da Vinci helped define the culture of the time. (In World History Series)

Masterpiece Mix. By Roxie Munro. 2017. 320p. Holiday House, $16.95 (9780823439126).

> An artist looks to 37 masterpieces for inspiration about what to paint and finally decides to borrow from each painting for a "Masterpiece Mix."

"POINTE" THE WAY

**was a dancing-school dropout. I don't remember one** routine, but I can demonstrate the five positions of ballet. There are pictures of me in a long line of five-year-olds performing three dances. None of us were together. There was the bluebird number (I lost a feather exiting the stage), The Little Fish in a Big Pond (I can still sing the song), and Little Toot (the costume was red, white, and blue, but there was nothing patriotic about the number). I tried dance class again when I was 35 years old. I dropped out before the spring performance. I didn't want to dance on the same stage as the students in the middle school where I worked. They were so much better (and looked better in the costumes). It's clear that my failure as a performer didn't influence my attitude toward dance. I love dance!

My town library had a limited collection of children's books, but it did have Noel Streatfeild's *Ballet Shoes.* I think I read it a dozen times when I was in fourth grade. The readers' comments about this novel on Amazon.com indicate that I wasn't the only young girl who became a dancer vicariously through Posy, Streatfeild's young heroine. I suspect that, like me, most of these readers never really became dancers.

Today, there are so many dance books available for young readers that a library might
resemble a dance studio. Watch children when
they discover *Ballerina Swan,* by Allegra Kent and
illustrated by Emily Arnold McCully. Many will
practice the five positions of ballet right there in
the library, along with the kids and swans in the
book. Tallulah and Beckett, the brother-and-sister
dancing team in *Tallulah's Solo,* by Marilyn Singer
and illustrated by Alexandra Boiger, capture the

heart of all budding dancers. It also celebrates a little brother's desire to
dance. *Miss Lina's Ballerinas and the Wicked Wish,* by Grace Maccarone and
illustrated by Christine Davenier, deals with the disappointment of not getting a desired role in a dance performance, something that most dancers face
at some point. Tony, one of the characters in the book, seems to be content to
be the only boy in a class of nine girls. There wasn't a boy in my dance class.

Dance! by Bill T. Jones and illustrated by Susan Kuklin, teaches young
readers the important role of the choreographer. I was an adult before I
knew that there was actually a person who created dance performances. *Ballet for Martha: Making Appalachian Spring,* by Jan Greenberg and Sandra Jordan and illustrated by Brian Floca; *Meet the Dancers: From Ballet, Broadway,
and Beyond,* by Amy Nathan; and *Alvin Ailey,* by Andrea Davis Pinkney and
illustrated by Brian Pinkney, are books that lead children toward the love of
dance, even if they have no desire or ability to actively participate on stage.

I became reacquainted with dance at the liberal arts college I attended.
We were required to attend all types of performances for cultural arts credit.
I always went to the shows by visiting dance companies. Most of my friends
groaned at the idea of spending an evening in this way. But the opportunity
to see professional dancers onstage was a real treat to me. Often the dances
were individually choreographed numbers, but there were also full ballets,
such as *Sleeping Beauty* and *Swan Lake.*

Dance is taught as a serious art form to most young children enrolled in
dance classes. Unlike my brief dancing days, children are now expected to
know actual ballet terms. I never knew *plié, pas de basque,* and *jeté* until I
became interested in studying ballet, not as a performer but as a fan. Now

dance is classically taught, and the dance books that children read use all the proper ballet terms.

Martha Graham once said, "Great dancers are not great because of their technique; they are great because of their passion." I believe that I'm a dancer at heart because of my passion for this art form. And I know that children are capable of making the same journey if they are exposed to dance through books and televised or live dance performances. To become a patron of dance is as important as becoming a performer. We just need to "pointe" the way.

November 2012

A Dance like Starlight: One Ballerina's Dream. By Karen Dempsey. Illus. by Floyd Cooper. 2014. 32p. Philomel, $16.99 (9780399252845). Set in Harlem in the 1950s, a young black girl has two dreams come true: she gets to study dance at the studio where her mother cleans and sews costumes; and she sees Janet Collins, the first black prima ballerina, dance.

Swan: The Life and Dance of Anna Pavlova. By Laurell Snyder. Illus. by Julie Morstad. 2015. 52p. Chronicle, $17.99 (9781452118901). This picture-book biography offers a glimpse at the early life of Anna Pavlova, but primarily focuses on her career as one of the world's greatest ballerinas and her iconic role as "The Dying Swan."

Where's the Ballerina? By Anna Claybourne. Illus. by Abigail Goh. 2017. 48p. Kane/Miller, $14.99 (9781610675154). A short synopsis of ten well-known ballets with colorful illustrations are presented as a puzzle in a *Where's Waldo* style.

TIMES A-CHANGIN'

 **s I reread *The Case for Loving: The Fight for Interracial Marriage*** (2015), written by Selina Alko, illustrated by Sean Qualls and Selina Alko, a particular line in the book stood out: "By now it was 1966, and the times they were a-changin.'" There was a lot happening in the 1960s, and singing the sweeping changes to victory was Bob Dylan, known for his political and philosophical song lyrics. He sang of race relations and war protests. And no one welcomed his messages more than Mildred and Richard Loving, whose interracial marriage was illegal in their home state of Virginia. Dylan wrote "The Times They Are a-Changin'" in 1964, three years before the U.S. Supreme Court ruled that the Virginia law was unconstitutional. Perhaps the nine justices took note of Dylan's third verse:

> Come senators, congressmen
> Please heed the call
> Don't stand in the doorway
> Don't block up the hall
> For he that gets hurt
> Will be he who has stalled.

It took courage for Mildred and Richard Loving to challenge the law, and there were people along the way who attempted to "block up the hall." Love won in the case of *Loving v. Virginia*, causing a shift in attitude toward marriage equality that extends to the 2015 Supreme Court decision that makes same-sex marriage legal.

In 1962 Dylan wrote "Blowin' in the Wind," a song that challenged Americans to think about racial discrimination. The 1964 Civil Rights Act created many changes and began moving the nation toward a more racially tolerant society. Maybe Congress again heard another of Dylan's questions: "How many times can a man turn his head / Pretending he just doesn't see?"

In the years since Dylan wrote that lyric, the nation has continued to deal with various degrees of racial and gender inequality. His music is as relevant today as it was when he was effecting change in the 1960s.

I came of age on the music of Bob Dylan, so I was thrilled to hear that he was awarded the 2016 Nobel Prize for Literature, though the news brought mixed reactions from around the world. Those happy with the choice felt that his lyrics are indeed poetry, but literary purists reacted differently. Journalists reported that Dylan is the "most radical choice in history." But history is always changing, and Sara Danius, permanent secretary of the Nobel Academy, stated, "Bob Dylan writes poetry for the ear." In 2008, the Pulitzer Prize jury awarded him a special citation for "his profound impact on popular music and American culture, marked by lyrical compositions of extraordinary poetic power." He has won 11 Grammy Awards, a Golden Globe Award, and an Academy Award, and he was the recipient of the 2012 Presidential Medal of Freedom.

"Lasting literary merit" is one of the criteria for the Nobel Prize in Literature. The fact that Dylan has provided people all over the world with thought-provoking and poetic lyrics for more than 50 years makes him a clear winner in the eyes of many. His work is timeless, and today my generation is introducing their grandchildren to Dylan's work. They bring out their guitars and ukuleles and sing: "The answer, my friend, is blowin' in the wind." They use picture books that set illustrations to the lyrics of Dylan's songs: *Forever Young* (2008), illustrated by Paul Rogers; *Man Gave Names to All the Animals* (2010), illustrated by Jim Arnosky; *Blowin' in the Wind* (2011), illustrated by Jon J. Muth; *If Dogs Run Free* (2013), illustrated by Scott Campbell; and *If Not for You* (2016), illustrated by David Walker. If children don't understand this man's contribution after reading these books, then offer them *Who Is Bob Dylan?* (2013), by Jim O'Connor and John O'Brien.

Perhaps the Nobel committee made an unconventional choice. But in Bob Dylan's own words, "The Times They Are a-Changin.'"

January 2017

Stand Up and Sing: Pete Seeger, Folk Music and the Path to Social Justice. By Susanna Reich. Illus. by Adam Gustavson. 2017. 48p. Bloomsbury, $17.99 (9780802738127).

Like Bob Dylan, Pete Seeger used powerful words in his music lyrics to champion social justice. This brief biography reveals how his musical career, which spanned six decades, effected societal changes.

PART 5

HOW FREEDOM TO READ DEFINES US

"Every time we listen to a student's opinion we have practiced and demonstrated the principles of intellectual freedom."

IT'S ABOUT
CONVERSATION

y passion for intellectual freedom began at home, not at school. Frankly I don't think that I ever had a teacher or a librarian who really wanted to know what I thought about a work of literature. But I had a father who not only wanted to know my thoughts, but wanted to challenge me intellectually by giving me the books that he read. These novels were by John Steinbeck, Erskine Caldwell, J. D. Salinger, Carson McCullers, and numerous other writers that have been censored. It never dawned on my father that I wasn't ready to read these books. He simply wanted to share them, and talk about them with me.

We talked about the conflict in *The Catcher in the Rye,* and how Holden Caulfield grew. We discussed his alienation and fear and his thoughts regarding the phoniness of the adults in his life. We compared Caulfield's fears to those of Frankie Addams in Carson McCullers' *The Member of the Wedding.* We related their feelings to those of most adolescents. We discussed the term "coming of age," and talked about the journeys of both of these characters. Why did Frankie Addams think that changing her name

would make things different for her? At what point did Holden Caulfield realize that he had the same faults that he saw in others? Scenes and words weren't censored; they were a natural part of our discussion.

This experience led me to develop a program at Greenville Middle School in the mid-1970s called "Communicate through Literature." Fifty parents gathered in the school library once a month to learn about the books their young adolescents were reading and to develop skills for discussing books with their children. No one seemed to shy away from the issues. In fact, the books provided a bridge that allowed them to deal with such tough issues as suicide, teenage sexuality, death, bullying, and drug and alcohol abuse. Before long, parents and students were reading together. Then Judy Blume read about the program and contacted me. She is the person who helped me see how this program actually promoted the principles of intellectual freedom.

I never thought too much about censorship until I met Judy Blume. It wasn't a part of my life. When I came to Greenville Middle School, *Are You There God? It's Me Margaret,* one of the most censored books at the time, had been out for two years. There wasn't a single copy in the school. I bought five copies for the library, and sold 150 copies in the school book fair in one afternoon. Kids were reading it. Parents were reading it. And while the book was being tried in major newspapers all across the nation, my students and their parents were discussing it together. Censors fear the unknown, often reacting to what the media has told them. My community's parents didn't react to *Margaret* because they knew the book and had used it to spark open and honest conversation with their young adolescents about a difficult topic. Before I realized it, I became a spokesperson for intellectual freedom and, in a proactive way, I began fighting in the censorship wars across the nation. By my side were Judy Blume, many of her young fans, and their parents.

The students in my school began to feel special because they were openly reading books that students in other schools in our city, and across the nation, didn't have access to. When a parent at another middle school in our district challenged *One Fat Summer* by Robert Lipsyte, my students wrote a letter to the materials review committee explaining why the book was important to them. The book was retained. *My Brother Sam Is Dead* by James Lincoln and

Christopher Collier was challenged in another school, and my students posed for the newspaper holding the book. Later, an editor of a newsletter in the Midwest wrote that she thought *Shiloh* by Phyllis Reynolds Naylor wasn't an appropriate book for children because Judd Travers, the character who abuses his dog, was too mean. My sixth-grade students became so angered by the editor's remarks that they wrote her letters. She printed all of them, and even admitted that these students helped her see that she was wrong.

Students began bringing me articles from newspapers and magazines about censorship. And I began teaching them about their First Amendment rights. Together, we became advocates for free speech. Students have opinions, and they want to be heard. Often their thoughts and opinions are enlightened. Students will reject what they aren't ready for if they are truly granted the freedom to read. Open and free. That's the kind of library I always wanted to manage, because that's how my father taught me.

I knew, early on, that the key element to an open and free library is trust. I began by getting to know my students as readers. I asked them to tell me what they liked or disliked about a particular novel. I never passed judgment on their thoughts, and I respected their ideas. They could reject books they didn't like. Soon students began requesting my help each time they wanted a

book to read. They would tell me, "You know what I like." (Wouldn't anyone respond this way when they think someone knows them so well that they can point them to just the right book?) I have a favorite quote from *Alice in Wonderland:* Alice says, "What is the use of a book without pictures and conversation?" I'm on the side of conversation. It is the only way to build a trusting relationship with students and their parents.

Censorship is about control. Intellectual freedom is about respect. Every time we listen to a student's opinion we have practiced and demonstrated the principles of intellectual freedom. Students want a forum where they may speak; the First Amendment grants them that right. Even school boards find it difficult to vote against an articulate student who is brave enough to stand up and fight for a book.

My father is no longer living, and I'm retired now. I will never forget the books he and I shared, and the conversations we had. Judy Blume is still by my side, and so are my students, all grown up now, and some of them are fighting censorship because they understand what it means to be intellectually free. My passion for intellectual freedom has defined my career, and I will continue to speak out on behalf of students because they deserve it.

Knowledge Quest, *a publication of the American Association of School Librarians, November/December 2007*

STUDYING THE FIRST AMENDMENT

his is America! Yet, according to statistics gathered by the ALA Office for Intellectual Freedom and the National Coalition against Censorship, there were more challenges brought against books in school and public libraries in 1994 than in any year since 1981. And so far, the challenges brought in 1995 indicate a steady rise. What is amiss in this "land of the free"? Is this "censorship war" about fear? Control? Power? Is it a fight between the "schooled" and the "un schooled"? The "sighted" and the "blind"? The "thinkers" and the "nonthink-ers"? How does this battle affect the education of our children? What kind of messages are we sending to them regarding their constitutional rights?

When I was in library school, there was a course called Censorship. This course surveyed books such as *Portnoy's Complaint, Of Mice and Men,* and *The Catcher in the Rye.* This was in the days before Judy Blume, Robert Corm-ier, Stephen King, R. L. Stein, Nancy Garden, and Alvin Schwartz. It was in the days when public libraries had more challenges than school libraries. It was five years before Steven Pico and his fellow high school students took the Island Trees school board to court for removing books from the school library. Most library school students took this censorship course for personal enjoyment; they never realized that fighting censorship could become a very real part of their job. Today, the battle is raging, and librarians are stumbling in their fight to win the war. The enemy is organized groups of people, from the right and the left, who are determined to gain power over what students read and learn. In some cities, library boards are under pressure to place ratings on books. In other places, students' names are tagged, at parental request, for restricted use of certain library materials. Frightened librarians are limiting young students to the "easy" books section, and they are requiring older students to bring written parental permission to read books such as Judy Blume's *Forever,* Mark Twain's *Huckleberry Finn,* Harper Lee's *To Kill a Mockingbird,* Alice Walker's *The Color Purple,* and Maya Angelou's *I Know Why the Caged Bird Sings.* Professionals are self-censoring in the selection process—making every effort to make "safe" book choices. These practices, however, aren't eliminating the problem; they are only amplifying the issue.

The problem is obvious. Censors want to control the minds of the young. They are fearful of the educational system because students who read learn to think. Thinkers learn to see. Those who see often question. And young people who question threaten the "blind" and the "nonthinkers." The answer is the classroom. As educators, we cannot, for the sake of the students, allow ourselves to be bullied into diluting the curriculum into superficial facts. We must talk about the principles of intellectual freedom. We must challenge students to think about the intent of our forefathers when they wrote the Bill of Rights. We must teach students about their First Amendment rights rather than restrict their use of certain books and materials. As educators, we must encourage students to express their own opinions while respecting the views of others.

By eighth grade, most students can define the Bill of Rights. They can, in a poetic fashion, render a memorized definition of the First Amendment. But do they really know how it affects their lives? Experience tells me that they don't. Teachers, through interdisciplinary units of study, can lead students toward understanding the implications of the First Amendment for the lives of all Americans. As librarians and library media specialists, we must realize that our task is much broader than raising public consciousness for First Amendment rights through Banned Books Week exhibits. Our professional role extends beyond removing all restrictions and barriers from the library collection. We must do these things, but we must also accept responsibility for creating a vital connection between the social studies and English curricula by preparing lessons on the First Amendment. We can go into the classroom and engage students in activities and discussion (suggestions are listed below) that will enable them to think about their personal rights and responsibilities provided by the Constitution. The appropriate time to make this connection is when students are already engaged in a study of the Constitution. Ask students to read and react to one of the contemporary novels that deal with censorship issues. Invite them to apply the situations in the novel to real life. Encourage them to debate the conflict presented in each novel. Allow them time to research various First Amendment issues. Provide a forum in which they can express their views regarding the subject of intellectual freedom. And help them understand their personal options regarding the use of books and materials that might offend them. Above all, grant them the opportunity to think, to speak, and to be heard. Classrooms and schools that foster this type of open atmosphere are sending a clear message: the First Amendment is important in school as well as in society at large. Thinkers, regardless of their views, make an important contribution to the American way of life. And thinkers are less likely to become censors.

SETTING THE SCENE

- Make available copies of the First and Fourteenth Amendments so that the class can read them. Ask the students to discuss what the First Amendment means to them. What would happen to our society if all ideas were censored? At what point does one relinquish one's First Amendment rights? How are the First and Fourteenth Amendments related?
- Display the following books: Maurice Sendak's *Where the Wild Things Are*, William Steig's *Sylvester and the Magic Pebble*, Judy Blume's *Are You There, God? It's Me, Margaret*, Lois Lowry's *The Giver*, Phyllis Naylor's *Shiloh*, and Paul Zindel's *The Pigman*. Ask the students how many of them have read these books. Then ask

them to identify reasons why some people find these titles objectionable. Solicit answers to the following: How does banning these books violate your First Amendment rights? What would you say to someone who told you that one of these titles was inappropriate for you to read? What can you do to protect your First Amendment rights?

ACTIVITIES

- Alvin Schwartz's *Scary Stories to Tell in the Dark* is among the top 10 most censored books in the United States today. Poll 25 adults, asking them if and why they feel scary stories are harmful to children and teenagers, then poll 25 of your peers, asking them the same question. Make a chart showing the results of each poll.

- Some parents feel that Halloween promotes evil and should not be celebrated in schools. Research the origin of Halloween and prepare a persuasive speech about why it should or should not be celebrated by children.

- Find out the procedure your school district has for dealing with challenged books and materials. Invite a member of the materials review committee or a member of the school board to speak to your class about local challenges. Prepare questions for the speaker.

- Research the purpose of each of the following organizations: the American Library Association's Office for Intellectual Freedom, the American Civil Liberties Union, the National Coalition against Censorship, the First Amendment Congress, and People for the American Way. Make brochures describing the mission of each organization. Include addresses and telephone numbers. Display the brochures in the school library.

- Read Ray Bradbury's *Fahrenheit 451* and Lois Lowry's *The Giver*. Write a paper discussing how each book represents thought control.
- Research Justice William Joseph Brennan's contribution to the Pico censorship case. Justice Brennan retired from the Supreme Court on July 20, 1990. Write a tribute to him from the "schoolchildren of America."
- Make a list of various types of censorship. Then draw a political cartoon regarding one type.
- Using a periodical index, locate as many articles as you can regarding book challenges in schools in the United States in the past five years. Draw a map of the United States and color in the states where you found challenges. Which state has the most challenges? How has each of the cases been resolved?
- Ballads and legends are often written about heroic people. Research John Peter Zenger's historic fight for freedom of the press and write a ballad or a legend about him (see Krensky's book in the bibliography).
- Banned Books Week is celebrated every September. The purpose of this observance is to make the public aware of the "horrors" and "harms" of censorship. Find out the dates of this special week and create a "Banned Books" exhibit for the school.

DISCUSSION

- Discuss the difference between a book challenge and censorship.
- How would your life be affected if we didn't have the First Amendment?
- Censorship is really about gaining "power" and "control" over what others believe and think. Many book challenges are brought by organized religious groups. Why does this happen? Why did our forefathers feel it necessary to include an amendment to the Constitution that guarantees freedom of religion to all Americans? Discuss the relationship between freedom of religion and freedom of expression.

- In the Pico censorship case (1982), one school board member said, "I would not dream of trying to take that book out of the public library. That would be censorship—and we are not censors." What are your feelings regarding this person's statement? Why would he think that removing a book from the school library would be censorship? How is the mission of a school library similar to that of a public library? How is it different?
- Interpret the following quote by Oscar Wilde: "The books that the world calls immoral are the books that show the world its own shame."
- In some cities, there is a movement to place ratings on books in school and public libraries. These ratings would be similar to the ones placed on movies and music. How are ratings on any work of art a form of censorship? How do you respond when you see that something is R-rated? Does it enhance your curiosity? What is it about human nature that makes us want to read the books that a person forbids us to read? Suggest ways that a family can deal with controversial books, movies, and music without forbidding their use.
- What is the meaning of "academic freedom"? Why is it important that educational institutions maintain this freedom?
- Technological advances have brought about new issues regarding censorship and intellectual freedom. How does the First Amendment protect user rights on the Internet and other online services? When "surfing the net," it is possible that you will come upon a conversation or graphics that offend you. How should you handle such a situation? Should online services be controlled or monitored for children? Why or why not?

FICTION

The Bookstore Mouse. By Peggy Christian. Illus. by
Gary A. Lippincott. 1995. 128p. Harcourt, $16
(0152002030).

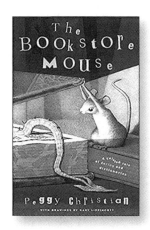

> Cervantes, a mouse who lives in an antiquarian
> bookstore, embarks on a great adventure while
> trying to elude Milo the cat. When Cervantes
> discovers the power of words, he finds a spe-
> cial way to deal with Milo, and they both live a
> more enlightened life.

The Rebellious Alphabet. By Jorge Diaz. Illus.
by Ivind S. Jorfald. 1993. 32p. Holt, $14.95
(0805027653).

> For older readers, this illustrated fable tells the story of an illiterate dic-
> tator who bans reading and writing but is outwitted by an old man who
> trains canaries to deliver printed messages to people.

The Trouble with Mothers. By Margery Facklam. 1989. 160p. Clarion, $13.95
(0899197736); Avon, paper, $2.95 (0380711397).

> Eighth-grader Luke Troy is devastated when his mother, a teacher, writes
> a historical novel that is considered pornography by some people in the
> community where they live.

The Day They Came to Arrest the Book. By Nat Hentoff. 1983. 160p. Dell, paper,
$3.99 (0440918146).

> Students in a high school English class protest the study of Mark Twain's
> *Huckleberry Finn* until the editor of the school newspaper uncovers other
> cases of censorship and in a public hearing reveals the truth behind the
> mysterious disappearance of certain library books and the resignation of
> the school librarian. Also note the 1988 film of the same name from Ruby-
> Spears Production, which is no longer distributed but is possibly available
> in local film libraries.

The Printer's Apprentice. By Stephen Krensky. Illus. by Madeline Sorel . 1995.
112p. Delacorte, $13.95 (0385320957).

> Using John Peter Zenger, a 1700s New York newspaper publisher, as his
> focus, Krensky unfolds a story about a young apprentice who witnesses the
> dramatic trial that changed the course of American journalism.

Memoirs of a Bookbat. By Kathryn Lasky. 1994. 192p. Harcourt, $11 (0152157271).

> Harper Jessup, an avid reader, runs away because she feels that her indi-
> vidual rights are threatened when her parents, born-again fundamentalists,
> launch a public promotion of book censorship.

Drummers of Jericho. By Carolyn Meyer. 1995. 336p. Harcourt/Gulliver, $11
(0152004416); paper, $5 (0152001905).

> When a 14-year-old Jewish girl joins the high school marching band and
> discovers that the band will play hymns and stand in the formation of a
> cross, she objects, raising major issues of individual rights.

Maudie and Me and the Dirty Book. By Betty Miles.1980. 144p. Knopf, o.p.; Bull-
seye, paper, $3.99 (0394825950).

> Eleven-year-old Kate Harris volunteers to read to first-graders, but her
> choice of book, *The Birthday Dog*, causes the children to ask questions
> about how puppies are born. When parents of the younger children raise
> an objection, the principal suspends the reading project, and Kate and her
> friends learn about censorship firsthand.

The Last Safe Place on Earth. By Richard Peck. 1995. 161p. Delacorte, $14.95
(0385320523).

> The Tobin family is satisfied that Walden Woods is a quiet, safe commu-
> nity in which to rear three children. Then, seven-year-old Mamie begins
> having nightmares after a teenage babysitter tells her that Halloween is
> evil, and Todd and Diana, sophomores in high school, witness an orga-
> nized group's attempt to censor books in their school library.

The Trials of Molly Sheldon. By Julian F. Thompson. 1995. 150p. Holt, $15.95
(0805033823).

> When high schooler Molly Sheldon begins working for her father in his
> eclectic general store in central Vermont, she faces First Amendment issues
> for the first time in her life. Moralists try to censor the books that her
> father sells, and Molly is accused of being a witch.

Save Halloween! By Stephanie S. Tolan. 1993. 176p. Morrow, $14 (0688121683).

> Sixth-grader Johnna Filkings gets caught up in researching and writing a
> class pageant about Halloween; much to her dismay, her father and uncle,
> who are fundamentalist ministers, disrupt the entire community by declar-
> ing Halloween evil.

NONFICTION

We the People: The Story of the United States Constitution since 1787. By
Doris and Harold Faber. 1987. 256p. Scribner, $15.95 (0684187531).

> A historical account of the writing of the Constitution and the adoption
> of the Bill of Rights, including a discussion of the responsibility of the
> Supreme Court as an interpreter of this fundamental document.

Board of Education vs. Pico. By John C. Gold. 1994. 96p. Twenty-First Century Books, $15.95 (068573093X).

> Gold traces the Pico case from its beginning in 1975 to the 1982 final Supreme Court decision that ordered the school board of the Island Trees Union Free School District No. 26 on Long Island, New York, to return nine books to the library shelves.

Adolescent Rights: Are Young People Equal under the Law? By Keith Greenberg. 1995. 64p. Holt/Twenty-First Century Books, $15.98 (0805038779).

> As Greenberg details adolescent rights from a historical and contemporary perspective, he invites readers to form their own conclusions regarding specific issues.

New York Times v. United States: National Security and Censorship. By D. J. Herda. 1994. 104p. Enslow, $17.95 (0894904906).

> Herda explores the 1971 landmark decision in which the Supreme Court decided in favor of the right of the *New York Times* to publish articles about the U.S. government's "secret war" against Vietnam and Cambodia.

Under 18: Knowing Your Rights. By Michael Kronenwetter. 1993. 112p. Enslow, $17.95 (0894904345).

> Focusing primarily on young people's rights while they are at school, this book also examines how these rights can best be established and protected.

The Bill of Rights: How We Got It and What It Means. By Milton Meltzer. 1990. 180p. HarperCollins, S14.89 (0690048076).

> This comprehensive discussion of the history of the Bill of Rights gives specific references to contemporary challenges against these ten amendments.

Censorship. By Judy Monroe.1990. 48p. Crestwood House, $10.95 (0896864901).

> A short, basic overview, in simple language, of the problems of censorship with regard to textbooks, movies, music, and children's books.

Freedom of Expression: The Right to Speak Out in America. By Elaine Pascoe. 1992. 128p. Millbrook, $15.90 (1562942557).

> Pascoe supplies a variety of historical and contemporary issues related to the First Amendment.

Tinker vs. Des Moines: Student Rights on Trial. By Doreen Rappaport. 1993. 160p. HarperCollins, S14.89 (0060251182); HarperCollins/Trophy, paper, $4.95 (0064461149).

> Part of the Be the Judge/Be the Jury series, this book deals with First and Fourteenth Amendment rights by re-creating the trial of John Tinker and

his classmates, who were suspended from school in 1965 for protesting the Vietnam War by wearing black armbands.

Censorship. **By Philip Steele. 1992. 48p. New Discovery Books, $12.95 (0027354040).**

This short, seven-chapter book looks at the history of censorship and its impact on American society.

Censorship: How Does It Conflict with Freedom? **By Richard Steins. 1995. 64p. Holt/Twenty-First Century Books, $15.98 (0805038795).**

The complex issue of censorship and how it affects and threatens our lives is addressed from historical and contemporary perspectives.

Free Speech: From Newspapers to Music Lyrics. **By Karen Zeinert. 1995. 128p. Enslow, $17.95 (0894906348).**

By introducing cases involving young people and then surveying what has happened with such issues in the past, Zeinert places today's censorship battles in a historical context.

September 1995

FICTION

Americus. **By M. K. Reed. Illus. by Jonathan David Hill. 2011. 224p. First Second, $18.99 (9781596436015).**

In this graphic novel, the Americus public library is under attack by a right-wing religious group, and ninth-grader Neal Barton finds himself in uncharted territory when he is thrust into an all-out defense of his favorite fantasy series.

Ban This Book. **By Alan Gratz. 2017. 243p. A Tom Doherty Associates Book, $16.99 (9780765385567).**

Amy Anne Ollinger discovers that her favorite book has been removed from the school library, and she sets out to lobby the school board to return it, along with other banned books, to the collection.

The Ninja Librarians. **By Jen Swann Downey. 2015. 400p. Source Books, $8.99 (9781492601807).**

Dorrie and her brother chase their dog into a closet in their local public library and discover the Ninja Librarians, a secret society formed to preserve the words of writers whose works have been censored through the ages. There is a cautionary message in this book of adventure, mystery, and fantasy.

NONFICTION

The Bill of Rights. **By Christine Taylor-Butler. 2007. 48p. Scholastic, $29.00 (9780531126271); paper, $6.95 (9780531147771).**

This book has an easy-to-read text and is heavily illustrated for young readers. Its very condensed history of the Bill of Rights leads to information about how these amendments apply to current issues. Sidebars, glossary, index augment the text. (A True Book Series)

Censorship. **By Ted Gottfried. 2005. 128p. Benchmark Books, $25.95 (9780761418832).**

Case studies explain current and often-volatile issues related to the Internet, book censorship, hate speech, and motion picture ratings. A center section called "You Be the Judge" asks readers to debate specific real-life scenarios. (Open for Debate Series)

Censorship, or Freedom of Expression? **By Nancy Day. 2005. 144p. Lerner, $25.26 (9780822526285).**

This book is peppered with anecdotal accounts of how people respond to censorship, and offers an examination of current issues related to movies, books, art, newspapers, the Internet, and government infringement on individual rights. (Pro/Con Series)

BECAUSE OF ALICE

PHYLLIS REYNOLDS NAYLOR'S ALICE BOOKS

**just reread the "Alice" series in order, and it was a** "Back to the Future" experience. It is obvious why this series has been so popular with girls for well over twenty years, and why it will continue its popularity for years to come. Naylor deals with every emotion, every thought, and every topic of concern to adolescent girls. And she is honest and open with the conflicts, solutions, and sometimes consequences they face. At the heart of all of her books is friendship and relationships. But, like all adolescents, Alice and her friends wonder about sex, and some of them, when they are 16 and 17, have their first sexual experience. This is one of the reasons the "Alice" series has been among the American Library Association's most challenged books from the 1990s to date.

THE START OF THE SERIES

Naylor never intended to write a series when she wrote *The Agony of Alice,* which was published in 1985. It turns out that Alice's agony as she struggles to make friends when she moves to Silver Springs, Maryland, is similar to that of many sixth-grade girls, regardless of whether they are the new kid

on the block like Alice. This novel was so wildly popular with young readers that Naylor wrote a sequel, *Alice in Rapture, Sort of.* It is now the summer before seventh grade, and Alice and her best friends Pamela and Elizabeth get their first boyfriends.

The fan mail began coming in at "Dear Abby" rate, and readers wanted to know when the next book would be available. And some readers had questions. They wanted to know about shopping for bras, getting their periods, and using tampons. They needed advice about how to talk to boys, when to kiss a boy, and how to deal with breakups. Some felt on the "outside" of the popular crowd and were desperate to belong to the "in" group—or any group at all.

At the dawn of the 1990s, Naylor realized that "Alice" needed to become a series. "I didn't want to write more than one book a year, and didn't want to be stuck in a sitcom where Alice is in the same class, the same year, forever. I agreed to start a series if Alice could grow a little older in every book."

This is what makes the series unique. In most other "series" novels, like Barbara Park's "Junie B. Jones," Beverly Cleary's "Ramona," and Lois Lowry's "Anastasia" and "Sam," the characters remain the same age. Therefore, these novels target a very narrow age range. Alice, on the other hand, keeps evolving: she gets her period, finds a steady boyfriend in a new boy named Patrick, dyes her hair green to express her individuality, fails her driver's tests, gets a part-time job, nervously awaits her SAT results, applies to colleges, and graduates high school.

She and her entire gang also come face-to-face with prejudice and bigotry and deal with other social issues like bullying, and a censorship incident in their high school library. There are school dances and slumber parties, but there is also sadness. One friend is killed in a car accident; another getting chemotherapy for cancer. One girl is faced with an unwanted pregnancy, another with a shotgun wedding her senior year in high school. There are plenty of triumphs and disappointments, but as Alice matures, she learns to cope with some of life's toughest matters one step at a time.

ALICE GROWS UP—AND ALSO GROWS YOUNGER

For many adolescents, it's easier to ask someone else's mom for advice than their own. But Alice's experience is different. Her mother died when she was five, so her upbringing is in the loving hands of her father and older brother, Lester. They are a close family, but there are certain things a girl needs to ask another woman. Aunt Sally, who lives in Chicago, is good for "long distance" advice, but she's a bit conservative and Alice doesn't want to broach subjects like boys and "sex" with her. Those questions she saves for her older cousin, Carol. Still, Alice longs for a stepmother to fill the void. She needs someone who can understand the female perspective and someone who can shop with her and help her dress for special occasions. Her dad is a good listener, but he's just not up for manicures and pedicures. Alice sets out on a mission to find her dad a wife and is ultimately successful in matching him with her seventh-grade language arts teacher, Sylvia Summers.

Sylvia is a good stepmother, but there is such a deep father-daughter bond that Alice's father remains the one to deal with most of the serious issues. There are curfews and consequences for broken rules, but Alice's father is a wise communicator. He poses questions that lead Alice to think about decisions, and he is also respectful of her answers when he confronts her with problems. After a serious conversation in *Almost Alice,* Alice's father tells her that he thinks she is "great, fantastic, trustworthy, loyal, helpful, friendly, courteous, and kind." And Alice is all of these things. She is her readers' best friend. She is the girl you would want to invite to a slumber party, have as a freshman roommate, share your most intimate secrets with, and trust for an honest opinion.

In 2002, Naylor responded to another demand from her fans. Parents asked that she consider writing Alice books for younger girls because so many of them wanted to read what their older sisters were reading. Naylor wrote three prequels that are about Alice in third, fourth, and fifth grade: *Starting with Alice, Alice in Blunderland,* and *Lovingly Alice.* She says, "I loved being able to connect with Alice when the loss of her mother in kindergarten was still so fresh; I loved seeing Lester as a more self-centered adolescent and their father's loneliness as Alice's personality is becoming better defined. I loved knowing that when the last Alice book is written—the 28th of the series—I will have followed the daughter I never had from age 8 to adulthood."

THE ALICE BLOG

Naylor says that it was her publisher's idea to bring "Alice" into the twenty-first century by creating an "Alice" blog. She was very open to the idea because it seemed the perfect way to communicate with her fans. You need only to visit the site and read some of the remarks and questions to realize what an impact Alice has had on the lives of girls in the past 20 years. Readers feel close enough to Alice's creator to share their most personal thoughts. Because of Alice, readers have found courage to confront issues of abuse, stand up to bullies, or deal with a controlling friend. Alice has traveled the world in plain view with some of her readers and has been kept safely hidden, like a personal diary, by others. Whether it's matters of the heart or something as seemingly frivolous as what dress to wear to a high school dance, adolescent readers know that everything about Alice is for real.

TALKING WITH PHYLLIS REYNOLDS NAYLOR

SCALES: Tell me about the birth of the Alice website.

NAYLOR: Several years into the series, I was getting swamped with letters from readers, and the publisher suggested a website (http://alicemckinley. wordpress.com) where we could post the answers to the most frequently asked questions, my biography, a list of the books to date in the order they were written, tips on writing, plus a chat room where kids could ask questions, I could respond, and so could other readers. We soon had problems with a few people who posted obscene messages in response to some readers' comments, and because neither the publisher nor I could police it 24/7, it was changed to readers' questions and comments, and my response only.

We envisioned the fan mail page as a place where readers could post suggestions and criticisms, and I could tell them about the research for various books as well as future titles. To our surprise, however, a huge number of comments were about personal problems. Because Alice had problems of her own, many of them around issues readers themselves were facing, girls—and sometimes guys—-felt that the Alice website was a place where they could be anonymous and ask the questions they couldn't ask anywhere else.

SCALES: Have readers' question on the website given you ideas for actual scenes, character dialogue, and themes to explore in the Alice books?

NAYLOR: Oh, yes. I've learned as much from them as they have from me. Just the language in their e-mail messages has been a new experience. I'd never heard of Spirit Week until readers told me about it, and most of the themes for each day of that week came from them. Molly's leukemia was another reader-inspired topic. Prank Day, Pep Rallies, worries about their bodies, fear of public speaking, the loss of a friend. . . . so many of their experiences mingled with memories of my own and were reshaped and tweaked to go in my books.

SCALES: The Alice series has been on ALA's Frequently Challenged Books list since the 1990s. Which was the first Alice book to be challenged and why?

NAYLOR: I believe it was *All but Alice* that was challenged by a school board in Wisconsin. I wanted an episode in the book in which a young teenage girl, acting out her independence, persists in arguing with her father even though she knows she's dead wrong. Alice has been persuaded by friends to join a fan club for a sleazy rock group known for their obscene lyrics, and when—in an argument with her father and older brother—she finds out just how disgusting the lyrics are (one of the group's song titles is "My Necrophiliac Lover"), she still can't admit that her father is right, and she accuses him of censorship for not buying any of their music for his store. (It's "selection," her father tells her.) The original complaining letter that reached the school board accused me of "promoting necrophilia."

SCALES: Do you ever hear from parents who just want to thank you for helping their daughter through puberty?

NAYLOR: I've had so many wonderful letters from parents—many of whom read these books aloud with their daughters. Here's one of my favorites: "I have a 17-year-old daughter and it occurred to me as we read the latest Alice book that you have been a godsend in helping me raise my kid. She is a better person because of Alice. Alice taught her to honor friendships, volunteer her time, and now to consider dignity in relationships. If I tried to guide her through these areas of her life, I would have failed. But when Alice speaks, my daughter listens. I am so grateful for your help. Thanks. P.S. When Alice got to college, will you please send her to a college I can afford?"

THE ALICE BOOKS

The bibliography below lists Phyllis Reynolds Naylor's Alice books according to Alice's age, beginning with the youngest books. Note that many of the titles are being re-released in paperback with new covers this year.

Starting with Alice. 2002. 192p. Atheneum, $15.95 (9780689843952); paper, $4.99 (9780689843969).

Alice in Blunderland. 2003. 208p. Atheneum, $15.95 (9780689843976); paper, $5.99 (9780689843983).

Lovingly Alice. 2006. 176p. Atheneum, $15.95 (9780689843990); paper, $5.99 (9780689844003).

The Agony of Alice. 1985. 144p. Atheneum, $17.95 (9780689311437); paper, $5.99 (9781416955337).

Alice in Rapture, Sort of. (1989) reissue, 1996. 144p. Atheneum, $17 (9780689805974); paper, $5.99 (9780689805974).

Reluctantly Alice. 1991. 192p. Atheneum, $16.96 (9780689316814); paper, $5.99 (9780689816888).

All But Alice. 1992. 160p. Atheneum, $16.95 (9780689317736); paper, $5.99 (9780689850448).

Alice in April. 1993. 176p. Atheneum, $16.00 (9780689318054); paper, $5.99 (9780689816864).

Alice In-Between. 1994. 160p. Aladdin paper, $4.99 (9780689816857).

Alice the Brave. 1996, 144p. Aladdin paper, $5.99 (9780689805981).

Alice in Lace. 1996. 144p. Atheneum, $17 (9780689803581); paper, $5.99 (9780689805974).

Outrageously Alice. 1997. 144p. Atheneum, $16.99 (9780689803543); paper, $5.99 (9780689805967).

Achingly Alice. 1998. 128p. Atheneum, $15.95 (9780689803550); paper, $5.99 (9780689863967).

Alice on the Outside. 2000 176p. Simon Pulse, $6.99 (9780689805943). Gr. 6–9.

The Grooming of Alice. 2000. 224p. Atheneum, $16.99 (9780689826337); paper, $4.99 (9780689846182). Gr. 6–9.

Alice Alone. 2001. 240p. Atheneum, $16 (9780689826344); paper, $5.99 (99780689851896).

Simply Alice. 2002. 240p. Atheneum, $16 (9780689859656); paper, $5.99 (99780689859656).

Patiently Alice. 2003. 256p. Atheneum, $15.95 (9780689826368); paper, $6.99 (9780689870736).

Including Alice. 2004. 288p. Atheneum, $15.95 (9780689826375); paper, $5.99 (9780689870743).

Alice on Her Way. 2005. 336p. Atheneum, $16.99 (9780689870903); paper, $6.99 (9780689870910). Gr. 8-up.

Alice in the Know. 2006. 288p. Atheneum, $16.99 (9780689870927); paper, $5.99 (9780689870934).

Dangerously Alice. 2007. 304p. Atheneum, $15.99 (9780689870941); paper, $6.99 (9780689870958).

Almost Alice. 2008. 272p. Atheneum, $16.99 (9780689870965); paper, $6.99 (9780689870972).

Intensely Alice. 2009. 288p. Atheneum, $16.99 (9781416975519); paper, $6.99 (9781416975540).

Alice in Charge. 2010. 352p. Atheneum, $16.99 (9781416975526); paper, $7.99 (9781416975557).

Incredibly Alice. 2011. 277p. Atheneum, $16.99 (9781416975533).

TALKING WITH
DORI HILLESTAD BUTLER

 n 2011, for the first time in a number of years, *And Tango Makes Three,* by Peter Parnell and Justin Richardson, wasn't on the Top 10 Most Challenged Books list, compiled by the American Library Association's Office for Intellectual Freedom. But sex and sexuality remain troublesome topics in school and public libraries across the nation. *My Mom's Having a Baby!* by Dori Hillestad Butler is currently number four on the list. The challenges to this factual picture book about childbirth were sparked after Fox News did a feature with a Texas babysitter who felt that the book was inappropriate for the nine-year-old girl in her care. Soon after the 2011 Top 10 Most Challenged Books list was published, I received an e-mail from Butler, who asked, "Did you see that I made the list?" Of course, I saw, and I was actually thrilled because now the book will become even more popular, as is often the case when a book is challenged. *My Mom's Having a Baby!* is an important book that answers questions that parents are some-

times uncomfortable broaching. In an interview, I asked Butler to respond to her newly crowned position on the Top 10 Most Challenged Books list.

SCALES: How did you react when you learned that *My Mom's Having a Baby!* **had landed on ALA's 2011 Most Challenged Books list?**
BUTLER: I was shocked. I knew the book had been challenged in some communities, but fourth-most-challenged book? Despite what would-be censors might say, *My Mom's Having a Baby!* is not a book "about sex." It's a book about a close-knit, loving family and their joy and anticipation prior to the birth of a second child. It does go one step further than similar books and answers the question that many children ask: How did that baby get inside Mom in the first place?

SCALES: What do you say to parents, or even librarians, who question whether this book should be in a library collection?
BUTLER: It should definitely be in a library collection. It makes me sad that some people don't want children to have accurate information about sex and reproduction, and it makes me angry that a few parents think they have a right to prevent other people's children from having access to that information. I know parents who use the book as a tool to begin discussing sexuality and reproduction with their children, and they want it available to them. Parents must make the decision for their own family. Librarians must serve all members of a community.

SCALES: Have you had face-to-face contact with kids who want to discuss your book? What are their reactions?
BUTLER: Yes. Some think it's a badge of honor to have a challenged book, and they are proud to know me. Others read the book and ask, "Why was this challenged?" I show them the two pages that are cited most often in challenges, and they ask, "That's it?" or "What's wrong with that?" Some laugh. One teenager told me her parents never talked to her about where babies come from. She's always gotten all of her information about sex from

books, and it makes her mad that people want to "get rid of all books that mention sex."

SCALES: Do you have other books that have been challenged in school and public libraries?

BUTLER: Yes, *Alexandra Hopewell, Labor Coach*, which is a humorous story about a fifth-grade girl's struggle to convince her mother she is responsible and mature enough to be her labor coach. When I was on an author visit, a school librarian told me that she "temporarily removed" the book from the library prior to my visit because she didn't want a student to take the book home and risk having a parent see it and get upset. She was worried that a parent might ask the school to rescind its invitation to me. *The Truth about Truman School* deals with cyberbullying from  the perspective of the bully, the bullied, and several bystanders. Before I visit schools, I send a survey on bullying and cyberbullying, and I incorporate the responses into my presentation so that the students, teachers, and administration can all see what kind of bullying problem they have at their school. But in some communities, some parents have flipped through the book and come across words like "gay" or "lesbian," and they have not only asked that their children not participate; they have tried to remove it from the curriculum. I also know of a teacher who refused to teach the book because he didn't like the fact that the characters questioned each other's sexual orientation.

SCALES: How has your view of censorship changed since making the most frequently challenged list?

BUTLER: I'm not sure my view of censorship has changed. What's changed is my willingness to stand up and be counted. I'm not sure any book is truly immune from censorship, and that frightens me.

SCALES: You are now in a "Sorority of Most Challenged" with writers like Judy Blume and Robie H. Harris, who are committed to fighting the

censors. What will you tell writers who face a first challenge to a book they've written?

BUTLER: I would advise a challenged writer who has been called upon to respond to the press to keep calm. Figure out the points you want to make, and just keep repeating them as calmly and concisely as you possibly can. I understand that when one of her books has been challenged, Robie H. Harris actually sends a letter to the school or library and asks how she can help. I want to learn from her about how to be better prepared to do something if my books continue to face challenges.

BIBLIOGRAPHY OF FACTS-OF-LIFE BOOKS

The following standout titles use a straightforward, sensitive approach to informing young people about sex and sexuality, and they have all been challenged in school or public libraries.

Amazing You: Getting Smart about Your Private Parts. By Gail Saltz. Illus. by Lynne Avril Cravath. 2005. 32p. Dutton, $16.99 (9780525473893); Puffin, paper, $6.99 (9780142410585).

   Illustrated with cartoon drawings and told in simple language, this book discusses the physical differences between girls and boys, how the body changes from infancy to adolescence, and basic information about reproduction.

How You Were Born. By Joanna Cole. Illus. by Margaret Miller. Rev. ed. 1984. 48p. HarperCollins, paper, $7.99 (9780688120610).

   This photo-essay traces the development of a fetus to the actual birth. How a baby is conceived isn't described. The color photos make the process seem real to a child who is asking first questions about childbirth.

It's Not the Stork: A Book about Girls, Boys, Babies, Bodies, Families, and Friends. By Robie H. Harris. Illus. by Michael Emberley. 2006. 64p. Candlewick, $16.99 (9780763600471); paper, $11.99 (9780763633318); e-book, $11.99 (9780763658632).

   This straightforward text, with humorous cartoon illustrations, emphasizes sexual health, including growth and development and how parents make babies. A short discussion called "Okay Touches, Not Okay Touches" sparks an understanding of the importance of the body and personal privacy.

It's Perfectly Normal: Changing Bodies, Growing Up, Sex, and Sexual Health. By Robie H. Harris. Illus. by Michael Emberley. Rev. ed. 2009. 96p. Candle wick, $22.99 (9780763626105); paper, $12.99 (9780763644840); e-book, $12.99 (9780763658649).

> Conception and puberty, birth control and AIDS, sexual intercourse, and heterosexuality and homosexuality are covered in this detailed text, which focuses on the biological and psychological questions that children have about sexual development. The cartoon illustrations, including small drawings of a bird and a bee sprinkled throughout the text, are scientific but humorous.

It's So Amazing! A Book about Eggs, Sperm, Birth, Babies, and Families. By Robie H. Harris. Illus. by Michael Emberley. 1999. 80p. Candlewick, $22.99 (9780763600518); paper, $12.99 (9780763613211); e-book, $12.99 (9780763658656).

> This honest approach to the way a baby is made, from the moment a sperm and an egg connect to the actual birth, includes realistic but funny cartoon illustrations, with the signature bird and bee creating dialogue throughout the text. Topics like love, gender, heterosexuality and homosexuality, sexual abuse, and HIV and AIDS are dealt with in a clear and sensitive way.

Mommy Laid an Egg!; or, Where Do Babies Come From? By Babette Cole. Illus. by the author. 1993. 40p. Chronicle, o.p.

> When nervous parents use ridiculous ways to teach their children the facts of life, the children set them straight by telling them all about sexual development, sexual relations, and childbirth, with their explanations illustrated by childlike, anatomically correct (but not graphic) cartoons.

My Mom's Having a Baby! By Dori Hillestad Butler. Illus. by Carol Thompson. 2005. 32p. Albert Whitman, $16.95 (9780807553442); paper, $6.95 (9780807553480).

> Elizabeth is eagerly awaiting the arrival of her baby brother and follows his month-by-month growth. She is curious about everything related to the pregnancy, but her biggest question—how the baby got inside her mom—is answered honestly, using correct anatomical terms. Cartoonlike illustrations of the baby's development, the mom's labor, and the actual birth expand the understanding of the text.

There's Going to Be a Baby. By John Burningham. Illus. by Helen Oxenbury. 2010. 48p. Candlewick, $16.99 (9780744549966).

> A mother explains to her curious son about the baby that she is expecting. He wonders

what they will call the baby and how the baby will change their lives, but he never questions why there is no father in the home. Illustrations of the mother and son's exchanges are interspersed with wild scenes from the boy's imagination.

What's Inside Your Tummy, Mommy? **By Abby Cocovini. Illus. by the author. 2008. 20p. Holt, paper, $8.95 (9780805087604).**

Using cartoon-style illustrations, Cocovini's book shows how an expectant mother helps her child understand the month-by-month development of the baby by comparing its size to everyday objects.

When You Were Inside Mommy. **By Joanna Cole. Illus. by Maxie Chambliss. 2001. 32p. HarperCollins, $7.99 (9780688170431).**

A young boy's parents tell him how happy they were on the day that he was born while presenting him with the facts about pregnancy and childbirth. The simplicity and sensitivity of the writing is well matched by the line and watercolor-wash illustrations.

Where Willy Went: The Big Story of a Little Sperm! **By Nicholas Allan. Illus. by the author. 2005. 32p. Knopf, e-book, $10.99 (9780375983801).**

Willy is one of 300 million sperm that live inside Mr. Brown, and more than anything, Willy wants the big prize of getting an egg. Although children might not glean many biological truths from the whimsical cartoon artwork, they will still enjoy the world of Allan's endearing, tadpole-like creatures.

Who Has What? All about Girls' Bodies and Boys' Bodies. **By Robie H. Harris. Illus. by Nadine Bernard Westcott. 2011. 32p. Candlewick, $15.99 (9780763629311).**

A brother and a sister change clothes for a day at the beach and become curious about the differences in girls' and boys' bodies. Humorous illustrations label the actual parts of the body so that children have no confusion about who has what.

September 2012

It's Perfectly Normal: Changing Bodies, Growing Up, Sex, and Sexual Health. By Robie H. Harris. Illus. by Michael Emberley.

Number 12 on the American Library Association's Top 100 Banned/Challenged Books List 2000–2009.

It's So Amazing! A Book about Eggs, Sperm, Birth, Babies, and Families. By Robie H. Harris. Illus. by Michael Emberley.

Number 37 on the American Library Association's Top 100 Banned/Challenged Books List 2000–2009.

Mommy Laid an Egg!; or, Where Do Babies Come From? By Babette Cole. Illus. by the author.

Number 77 on the American Library Association's Top 100 Banned/Challenged Books List 1990–2000.

THREE BOMBS,
TWO LIPS, AND
A MARTINI GLASS

f you had asked me a year ago what bombs, lips, and martini glasses have in common, I would have answered, "A fraternity party." Now I have a different answer. It's called Common Sense Media. This not-for-profit Web-based organization is in the business of using a "rating" system to review all types of media that target children, but their "ratings" of books are especially disingenuous. They claim that they want to keep parents informed. Informed about what? What their children should read or what they shouldn't read?

This isn't the first time that an organization has used the World Wide Web to influence parental opinions about children's literature. Parents against Bad Books in Schools and a number of right-wing groups have been at work for years trading "forbidden" lists of children's books. It's never been clear who decides what titles make the lists. Now, Common Sense Media joins the long list of organizations that think they know what is best for children. The frightening part about this group is that they have a marketing strategy to convince parents and even teachers and librarians that "rating" materials is a "good" thing. But good turns to bad when reviewers aren't really reviewers, and the focus is on what to watch out for.

Common Sense Media claims that it is about "media sanity, not censorship," but after a long meeting with their editor in chief, I remain puzzled about how they define "media sanity." As a company, it is free to do what it pleases, but the belief that "media has truly become the 'other parent'" and its approach to media guidance display great disrespect for children and their families, not to mention the disdain it demonstrates to librarians who are trained to provide reading guidance to families.

Children deserve to be challenged intellectually, and they deserve to be the judges of the books that suit them. Most children will reject books they aren't ready for, and they don't need adults to help them with that decision. Common Sense Media assumes that all parents want to police what their kids are reading, and they use the following emoticons as warnings: bombs for violence, lips for sex, #! for language, $ for consumerism, and martini glasses for drinking, drugs, and smoking.

In addition to rating books in these five categories, the site also decides whether books have any educational value and redeeming role models. Finally, they give titles an overall "on," "off," or "iffy" rating. For example, *The Evolution of Calpurnia Tate,* by Jacqueline Kelly, a 2010 Newbery Honor Book, is rated "on" for ages 12 and up. My bet is that there are plenty of 9-year-olds waiting in line for the book. It gets one bomb for violence because of a description of a Civil War battle and reportage of a servant who is pitchforked to death; a lip because Calpurnia's older brother is courting and animals on the farm mate; one #! because Calpurnia's grandfather curses; and two martini glasses because her grandfather drinks whiskey and port daily. There are further warnings under "What Parents Need to Know." What Common Sense Media doesn't tell you is that 11-year-old Calpurnia is a spunky kid who would rather be collecting scientific specimens with her grandfather than learning to become a housewife.

Common Sense Media clearly doesn't know how to deal with young-adult readers. Filter the site by "iffy" books and ages 15–up, and you are left holding frowning faces, bombs, lips, "#!," and martini glasses. *Looking for Alaska,* by John Green, winner of the 2006 Michael L. Printz Award, is rated "iffy" for ages 15–18. *Booklist* graded this book at grades 9–12, and even the "Average Rating" by kids, parents, and educators on the Common Sense site

recommends Green's book for ages 12–up. Regardless of what these readers say, the Common Sense Media reviewer warns, "Parents need to know that this book hits all the controversial pulse points: drinking, (not graphic) sex, bad language, and smoking, including marijuana smoking."

In May 2010, the National Coalition against Censorship, American Library Association's Office for Intellectual Freedom, National Council of Teachers of English, Association of American Publishers, Pen American Center, International Reading Association, American Booksellers Foundation for Free Expression, Authors Guild, and Society of Children's Book Writers and Illustrators sent a joint letter to the editor in chief and the CEO of Common Sense Media that outlined the following concerns with the company's rating system: (1) the implication that certain kinds of content are inherently problematic; (2) the negative attitude toward books; and (3) the potential that the ratings will be used to remove valuable literature from schools and libraries. A meeting was held with the editor in chief, and questions were raised about why books such as Markus Zusak's *Book Thief* and Annika Thor's *Faraway Island,* both set during the Holocaust, and Laurie Halse Anderson's *Chains,* set during the American Revolution, weren't given any "educational value." The editor in chief had no clear answers, but those books have now been awarded "educational value" on Common Sense Media's site. It is clear to the nine organizations that are working hard to protect children and young adults' freedom to read that Common Sense Media is a moving target, and its piecemeal response to such questions won't fix what is at heart a misguided and dangerous concept.

While Common Sense Media isn't censoring anything, it is providing a tool for censors. There is already a documented case in the Midwest where a book was removed from a school library based solely on a Common Sense review. Common Sense Media allows users to filter books by "on," "off," and "iffy" ratings. And reviewers are instructed to point out anything "controversial." Such warnings encourage site browsers to take things out of context instead of looking at books as a whole.

Bombs, lips, and martini glasses! Indeed, let them be a warning. We must be proactive in helping parents understand that rating books is dangerous. Otherwise, more censorship bombs are sure to explode.

WHAT PARENTS NEED TO KNOW

Parents need to know that this book hits all the controversial pulse points: drinking, sex, bad language, and smoking, including marijuana smoking, but as Michael Cart, former president of the Young Adult Library Services Association and former chair of the Michael L. Printz committee, says in the publisher's discussion guide, "There is nothing (I repeat, NOTHING) gratuitous in this book. Everything in it serves to define character, give style to voice, and develop theme." Indeed, this award-winning book is

Continue reading ⌄

USER REVIEWS

PARENTS	KIDS
Adult Written by sadmom April 23, 2013	age 15+ ★★★★☆
	WATCH OUT! Holy cow. Be aware this book is available in many MIDDLE SCHOOLS, even though it contains a first-person account of oral sex as well as descriptions of porn fi... Flag as inappropriate

August 2010

Content has been revised to reflect minor changes in the way Common Sense Media rates books (www.booklistreader.com/2016/03/31/libraries/three bombs-two-lips-and-a-martini-glass-revisited.)

IT'S SEPTEMBER

n early September of my seventh-grade year, Mrs. Till, my literature teacher, issued a textbook that was simply an anthology of abridged works, including *The Thread That Runs So True,* by Jesse Stuart; *The Old Man and the Sea,* by Ernest Hemingway; and *Little Britches: Father and I Were Ranchers,* by Ralph Moody. The text included a few poems, like "Annabel Lee," by Edgar Allan Poe, and "Trees," by Joyce Kilmer. Even the Gettysburg Address was included in the poetry section. I was acutely aware, even then, that there wasn't a single entry by a woman or anyone of color. Where was Pearl Buck's *The Good Earth*? Or some of Eudora Welty's short stories? And why weren't there poems by Paul Lawrence Dunbar and Langston Hughes? Who edited these textbooks?

There were questions and activities at the end of each textbook entry. What was the theme of the story? Discuss the author's style of writing. Write about the symbolism in the poem. We weren't prepared to respond, though, because Mrs. Till never led a discussion about the works. Instead, we spent class time reading aloud. She would call on a student in the front row and proceed down the rows until the last student in the class had a turn. None of us paid attention to what was being read because we were reading ahead to be prepared when our turn came. On the day we read *Little Britches* (at least I think that was the story), I read ahead and discovered a passage where a dog "wet on the floor." I held my breath that Mrs. Till wouldn't call on me to read that. But that is exactly the passage I was asked to read. The class roared with laughter. I was humiliated.

If I were a student today, that passage would not affect me at all. I could read "peed on the floor" and probably get no laughter. Children are very capable of responding appropriately to entire works of literature, and if taught, they know not to take words out of context, and that bodily functions are normal and necessary. I have read aloud *Shiloh,* by Phyllis Reynolds Naylor, and didn't get a single gasp when I read that Judd Travers called his dogs "one, two, three, dammit." Nor did I get a single giggle when we read aloud *The Giver,* and Jonas experienced "stirrings." Some got it, but others didn't. When we read *The Watsons Go to Birmingham—1963,* by Christopher Paul Curtis, students laughed in all the right places and grew quiet and solemn at the horror of the bombing of the Sixteenth Baptist Church in Birmingham. It was an emotion they needed to feel. Yet there are adults in this nation who say children can't handle such works. Some want to label books if they are "controversial" and place them on restricted shelves. And some organized groups produce websites that call for the outright banning of certain titles.

Children are fortunate to have writers who believe in being honest with their readers, and to learn from educators and librarians who respect their students by bravely exposing them to all kinds of literature. This may include Junie B. Jones, who uses bad grammar; Captain Underpants, who flies around in his "tighty whities"; and Greg Heffley, who acts a bit wimpy. It may include works by Sherman Alexie, Jacqueline Woodson, Matt de la Peña, Jack Gantos, Mary Downing Hahn, and Cynthia Kadohata. Give them books by all of these writers, but don't forget Julie, who was lost on the Alaskan tundra; Tim Meeker, whose brother and father were on opposite sides of the American Revolution; Jesse Aarons, who had to deal with grief far too soon;

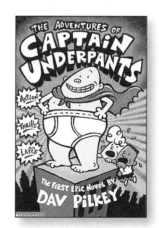

Lucky Trimble, who desperately needed a mother; and little Tango, who was so lovingly reared by two penguin dads.

It's September, a time we celebrate Banned Books Week. This is an opportunity to also celebrate young readers by asking them to read and think deeply about the issues that so many adults want to suppress. Only then might they read aloud "wet on the floor" to no laughter at all.

September 2015

INDEX

#

13 (Howe), 36

1900s and 1910s, 60–61, 65, 69, 143

1960s, 24–25, 31–32, 34, 98–99, 166–167

The 1964 Freedom Summer (Felix), 105

A

Abramovitch, Ilana, 86–88

activities, 15, 20, 34, 58, 113–114, 131–132, 139–140, 178–179

Adler, David A., 45, 92, 106

Adoff, Arnold, 110

Adolescent Rights (Greenberg), 183

adoption, 21–23

African American history, 20, 97–108, 109–114, 131, 153–155

Afternoon of the Elves (Lisle), 146

The Agony of Alice (Naylor), 186–187, 191

Al Capone Does My Shirts (Choldenko), 4, 67–68

An Album of Women in American History (Ingraham), 62

Alexandra Hopewell, Labor Coach (Butler), 195

Alice Paul and the Fight for Women's Rights (Kops), 63

"Alice" series, 186–192

Alko, Selina, 109, 113, 166

Allan, Nicholas, 198

Almost Astronauts (Stone), 123, 126

Amazing You (Saltz), 196

"Ambassador of the World," 44–46

Amelia Lost (Fleming), 51

America in the 1900s and 1910s (Callan), 69

American history, 52–54, 55–63, 69, 72–81, 97–108, 109–114

American Library Association (ALA), 175, 178, 186, 193, 199, 202

Americus (Reed), 184

Anderson, Laurie Halse, 142, 203

Anne of Green Gables (Montgomery), 12, 21, 44

Antonio's Apprenticeship (Morrison), 160

Archer, Jules, 61

Architecture According to Pigeons (Tailfeather), 135

architecture and construction, 135–140

Arenas, Jose Fernandez, 159

Aretha, David, 106, 107

Armstrong, Jennifer, 92

Arnold, Elana K., 6–15

Art and Architecture (Tomecek), 136

art and artists, 136, 140, 153–155, 156–162, 166–168

Art Dog (Hurd), 159

Ashby, Ruth, 61

Astronauts (Goldstein), 123

Auma's Long Run (Odhiambo), 143

author interviews

    Elana K. Arnold, 6–13

    Dori Hillestad Butler, 189–191, 193–197

author interviews *(cont'd)*
  Angela Cerrito, 85–93
  Gennifer Choldenko, 64–69
  Phyllis Reynolds Naylor, 189–191
  Susan Goldman Rubin, 97–108
  Graham Salisbury, 72–81
  Steve Sheinkin, 128–134
  Rita Williams-Garcia, 24–31
Averbeck, Jim, 112
Avi, 19, 37

B
A Bag of Marbles (Joffo), 92
Ballerina Swan (Kent), 164
ballet, 163–165
Ballet Shoes (Streatfeild), 163
Ballot Box Battle (McCully), 60
Ballots for Belva (Bardhan-Quallen), 51
Ban This Book (Gratz), 184
Bang (Flake), 18
Banned Books Week, 177, 179, 184, 199,
  206. *See also* censorship
Barack Obama (Grimes), 110
Bardhan-Quallen, Sudipta, 51
Barnard, Bryn, 142
Bartoletti, Susan Campbell, 83, 143
Baseball Crazy (Mercado), 36
Baseball in April and Other Stories (Soto), 36
"Because of Alice," 186–192
Because of Shoe and Other Dog Stories
  (Martin), 36
Bemelmans, Ludwig, 21, 44
Bender, Michael, 159
Benjamin, Ali, 14
Benjamin, Floella, 112
Big Annie of Calumet (Stanley), 63
Bill of Rights, 116, 176, 183, 185
The Bill of Rights (Meltzer), 183
The Bill of Rights (Taylor-Butler), 185
Billions of Bricks (Cyrus), 140
biographies, 52–54
bipolar disorder, 145–150
Bird, Betsy, 38
Black, White, Just Right! (Davol), 110
Black History Month, 153–155. *See also*
  African American history
Black Is Brown Is Tan (Adoff), 110
blogs
  "Alice" series, 189
  Interesting Nonfiction for Kids, 131
Bloomers! (Blumberg), 60
Blos, Joan, 60

The Blossoming Universe of Violet Diamond
  (Woods), 110
"Blowin' in the Wind" (Dylan), 167–168
Blue Skin of the Sea (Salisbury), 77, 81
Blumberg, Rhoda, 60
Blume, Judy, 172, 174, 175–176, 178,
  195–196
Board of Education vs. Pico (Gold), 183
Bomb (Sheinkin), 128–133
Book Links magazine, ix–xii, 16, 31–32, 156
The Book Thief (Zusak), 84, 203
Booklist, ix–xi, 201
books
  challenged and banned, 186, 190,
    193–195, 199 (*see also* censorship)
  exploring the world through, 44–46
  getting sidetracked by, 39–40
  ratings of, 180, 200–203
The Bookstore Mouse (Christian), 181
Bornstein, Michael, 84
Bovsun, Mara, 37, 83
The Boxcar Children (Warner), 22
Breaking Barriers (Archer), 61
Breathing Room (Hayles), 143
*Brendan Buckley's Universe and Everything in
  It* (Frazier), 110–111
Bridge to Terabithia (Paterson), 12, 13
Brill, Marlene Targ, 61
Brooklyn Doesn't Rhyme (Blos), 60
Bryant, Jennifer, 61, 155
Bubonic Panic (Jarrow), 69
Bud, Not Buddy (Curtis), 18, 22
Burleigh, Robert, 126–127, 155
Burnett, Frances Hodgson, 21–22, 142
Burningham, John, 197–198
Butler, Dori Hillestad, 193–197
Byars, Betsy, 37

C
Callan, Jim, 69
Calvin Coconut series, 78–80
The Case for Loving (Alko), 109, 113–114,
  166
Castle (Macaulay), 136
The Catcher in the Rye (Salinger), 171, 175
Cathedral (Macaulay), 136
The Cats in Krasinski Square (Hesse), 92
censorship, 171–174, 175–185, 190,
  193–199, 200–203, 204–206
Censorship (Gottfried), 185
Censorship (Monroe), 183
Censorship (Steele), 184

Censorship (Steins), 184

Censorship, or Freedom of Expression? (Day), 185

Cerrito, Angela, 85–93

Chains (Anderson), 203

challenged books, 186, 190, 193–195, 199. *See also* censorship

Challenger shuttle, 123, 132–133

Chasing Orion (Lasky), 143

Chasing Secrets (Choldenko), 64–69

Chasing the Milky Way (Moulton), 146

children. *See* students

child-rescue operations, 85–93

Choldenko, Gennifer, 4, 64–69

Chomp (Hiaasen), 4

Christian, Peggy, 181

The Chronicles of Harris Burdick (Van Allsburg), 36–37

Cinnamon Baby (Winstanley), 111

citizenship, 115–117

The Civil Rights Act of 1964 (Wright), 106

civil rights movement, 97–108, 109, 113–114, 131, 167

classroom activities, 15, 20, 34, 58, 113–114, 131–132, 139–140, 178–179

Claybourne, Anna, 165

Cocovini, Abby, 198

Cohen-Janca, Irene, 93

Cole, Babette, 197, 199

Cole, Joanna, 196, 198

Collard, Sneed B., 155

Columbus and the World Around Him (Meltzer), 160

Common Core State Standards, x–xi, 131

Common Sense Media ratings, 200–203

Computer Graphics (Kettelkamp), 159–160

construction and architecture, 135–140

Cornille, Didier, 138

Corsi, Jerome R., 159

Couloumbis, Audrey, 146

Crazy (Nolan), 146

Cumming, Robert, 159

Curious Constructions (Hearst), 140

Curlee, Lynn, 138

Currie, Stephen, 107

Curtis, Christopher Paul, 5, 14, 18, 22, 37, 154, 205

Cyrus, Kurt, 140

D

dance, 163–165

Dance! (Jones), 164

A Dance like Starlight (Dempsey), 165

Dash, Joan, 61

Davidson, Rosemary, 159

Davis, Kathryn Gibbs, 137

Davol, Marguerite W., 110

Day, Nancy, 185

The Day the Women Got the Vote (Sullivan), 63

The Day They Came to Arrest the Book (Hentoff), 181

death and grief, 6–15

Death with Dignity Act, 15

Dempsey, Karen, 165

dePaola, Tomie, 116

depression, 146–150

The Diary of Anne Frank (Frank), 45, 70–71

Diaz, Jorge, 181

Diggs, Taye, 111

discrimination, 28, 76, 103, 105, 167. *See also* civil rights movement

discussion questions, 19–20, 33–34, 57–58, 148–149, 158, 179–180

disease, 64–69, 141–143, 144–150

The Dollmaker of Krakow (Romer), 93

Down, Susan Brophy, 92

Downey, Jen Swann, 184

Dragonwings (Yep), 69

Drummers of Jericho (Meyer), 182

Duffy, James, 60

Dylan, Bob, 166–168

E

Eggers, Dave, 138

Ehrlich, Esther, 14, 143, 147

elections, 115–117

Elish, Dan, 133

Enrique's Journey (Nazario), 32

Everyone Paints (Rubin), 155

The Evolution of Calpurnia Tate (Kelly), 201

extension activities, 15, 20, 34, 58, 113–114, 131–132, 139–140, 178–179

Extraordinary People of the Civil Rights Movement (Hardy), 106

Eyes of the Emperor (Salisbury), 72–73, 76–77, 81

F

Faber, Doris and Harold, 182

Facklam, Margery, 181

facts-of-life books, 196–199

Faith, Hope and Ivy June (Naylor), 4

Fallout (Krisher), 134

Fallout (Strasser), 134
families
    adoption by, 21–23
    different kinds of, 3–5, 19
    father-son relationships in, 16–20
    interracial, 109–114, 166–167
    mental illness in, 144–150
Far from Fair (Arnold), 6–15
Faraway Island (Thor), 95, 203
father-son relationships, 16–20
Favorite Stories for Sharing (Avi), 37
Feinstein, Stephen, 106
Felix, Rebecca, 105
Feynman, Richard, 129–130, 132–133
A Finders-Keepers Place (Leal), 146
Finding the Worm (Goldblatt), 13
Fireside, Harvey, 107
First Amendment, 173–174, 175–185. *See also* intellectual freedom
The First Women Who Spoke Out (Levinson), 62
Fish (Matthews), 95
Fitzhugh, Louise, 5
Flake, Sharon, 18
Fleming, Candace, 51
Fletcher, Marty, 133
Footer Davis Probably Is Crazy (Vaught), 144–146, 148–149
Forward into Light (Meyers), 61
The Fourteenth Goldfish (Holm), 13–14
Frank, anecdote about, 153–155
Frank, Anne, 45, 70–71, 96, 104
Frazier, Sundee T., 110–111, 112
Free Speech (Zeinert), 184
freedom, intellectual, 171–174, 175–185, 193–199, 200–203, 204–206
Freedom of Expression (Pascoe), 183
Freedom School, Yes! (Littlesugar), 105
Freedom Summer, 97–108
Freedom Summer (Aretha), 106
Freedom Summer (Wiles), 105
The Freedom Summer Murders (Mitchell), 106
The Friendship Doll (Larson), 46
Fritz, Jean, 46, 52–54, 55–59, 116
Funny Girl (Bird), 38

G

The Gadget (Zindel), 132
Geller, Mark, 19
gender gap, 126
Genevieve's War (Giff), 93
George Bellows (Burleigh), 155

Gephart, Donna, 117, 150
Get Well Soon (Halpern), 150
Getting Near to Baby (Couloumbis), 146
Giff, Patricia Reilly, 22, 46, 71, 93, 143
The Giver (Lowry), 43, 178, 179, 205
The Glorious Impossible (L'Engle), 160
Glory Be (Scattergood), 105
Gold, John C., 183
Gold, Susan Dudley, 61, 113
Goldblatt, Mark, 13
The Golden Gate Bridge (Stanborough), 136
Goldstein, Margaret J., 123
Gone Crazy in Alabama (Williams-Garcia), 29, 31
Gonzales, Doreen, 133
"Gotcha Day," 21–23
Gottfried, Ted, 185
Grace Hopper (Wallmark), 127
Gratz, Alan, 96, 184
The Great Explainer (LeVine), 132–133
Great Painters (Ventura), 161
Green, John, 201–202
The Green Glass Sea (Klages), 132
Greenberg, Keith, 183
grief, 6–15
Grimes, Nikki, 30, 110, 112
Guarnaccia, Steven, 138
Guys Read (Scieszka), 37

H

Halloween, views on, 178, 182
Halpern, Julie, 150
Hamer, Fannie Lou, 98–99, 102–103, 106–107
Hamilton, Margaret, 127
Hardy, Sheila and P. Stephen, 106
Haring, Kay A., 155
Harriet the Spy (Fitzhugh), 5, 12
Harrington, Karen, 5, 147
Harris, Annie, 161
Harris, Robie H., 195–199
Harvey, Jeanne Walker, 140
Hattie Ever After (Larson), 69
Hayles, Marsha, 143
health, public, 64–69, 141–143
Hearst, Michael, 140
Heller, Max and Trude, 94–96
The Hello, Goodbye Window (Juster), 111
Hentoff, Nat, 181
Her Story (Ashby and Ohm), 61
Herda, D. J., 183
A Hero and the Holocaust (Adler), 92

Heroes for Civil Rights (Adler), 106
Hesse, Karen, 92
Hey 13! (Soto), 35–36
Hiaasen, Carl, 4
Hiding from the Nazis (Adler), 92
The Higher Power of Lucky (Patron), 32
Hiranandani, Veera, 147
historical fiction, writing process for, 65–66,
    75–76, 86–91
history
    African American, 20, 97–108,
        109–114, 131, 153–155
    American, 52–54, 55–63, 69, 72–81,
        97–108, 109–114
    Jewish, 37, 71, 82–84, 85–93, 94–96,
        203
history celebrations
    Black History Month, 153–155
    Women's History Month, 49–51
A History of Voting Rights (Orr), 106
Hodges, Margaret, 62
Holiday House website, 38, 93, 108
Holinstat, Debbie Bornstein, 84
Holm, Jennifer L., 13, 43
Holocaust, 37, 71, 82–84, 85–93, 94–96,
    134, 182, 203
Holocaust Memorial Museum, 82–84, 94
Homesick (Fritz), 46, 53
The Hoover Dam (Zuehlke), 136
Hope (Monk), 111
Hopkinson, Deborah, 137, 142
Horris, Nathaniel, 159
House of the Red Fish (Salisbury), 71, 72,
    77, 81
"How Do We Say Thank You, Jean Fritz?,"
    52–54
How You Were Born (Cole), 196
Howe, James, 36
Humming Whispers (Johnson), 146–147
Hurd, Thatcher, 36, 159

I

I, Juan de Pareja (Treviño), 45
I Am Malala (Yousafzai), 96
If I Built a House (Van Dusen), 136–137
illnesses, 64–69, 141–143, 144–150
immunizations, 142–143
In My Hands (Opdyke and Armstrong), 92
In Our Mother's House (Polacco), 4, 111,
    114
informational books, evolution of, 131
Ingraham, Claire and Leonard, 62

Inspiring African American Civil Rights Leaders
    (Feinstein), 106
intellectual freedom, 171–174, 175–185,
    193–199, 200–203, 204–206
Interesting Nonfiction for Kids blog, 131
Internet resources. *See* websites
interracial marriage, 109–114, 166–167
interviews. *See* author interviews
Irena Sendler (Down), 92
*Irena Sendler and the Children of the Warsaw
    Ghetto* (Rubin), 93, 104
Irena's Jars of Secrets (Vaughan), 93
It Ain't All for Nothin' (Myers), 32
The Italian Renaissance (Osman), 161
"It's About Conversation," 171–174
"It's Not My War," 70–71
It's Not the Stork (Harris), 196
It's Perfectly Normal (Harris), 196–197, 199
"It's September," 204–206
It's So Amazing! (Harris), 197, 199

J

J. Robert Oppenheimer (Scherer and
    Fletcher), 133
Jacob Lawrence (Collard), 155
Jacobson, Jennifer Richard, 147
James Forman and the SNCC (Uschan), 107
Japanese Americans, 71, 72–77
Jarrow, Gail, 69
Jewish Historical Institute, 86–88
Jews and Jewish history, 37, 71, 82–84,
    85–93, 94–96, 134, 182, 203
Joffo, Joseph, 92
Johnson, Angela, 22, 146–147, 154
Johnson, Norma, 62
Jones, Bill T., 164
Jones, Traci L., 147
Journey (MacLachlan), 32
Just Imagine (Cumming), 159
Juster, Norton, 111

K

Kadohata, Cynthia, 14, 46, 71, 205
Keenan, Sheila, 62
Keith Haring (Haring), 155
Kelly, Jacqueline, 201
Kent, Allegra, 164
Kent, Rose, 147
Kettelkamp, Larry, 159–160
The Key to Renaissance Art (Arenas), 159
Kidd, Ronald, 132
King, Casey, 107

Kinsey-Warnock, Natalie, 33
Kira-Kira (Kadohata), 14
Klages, Ellen, 132
Knowledge Quest, xi, 174
Koertge, Ronald, 18, 36
Konigsburg, E. L., ix–x, 156–160
Kops, Deborah, 63
Kraft, Betsy Harvey, 62
Krensky, Stephen, 181
Krisher, Trudy, 134
Kronenwetter, Michael, 183

L

Labrecque, Ellen, 139
Lafferty, Peter, 160
Langmead, Donald, 137
Larson, Kirby, 46, 69
Lasky, Kathryn, 60, 126, 143, 181
Lassieur, Allison, 162
The Last Mission (Mazer), 71
The Last Safe Place on Earth (Peck), 182
Lawlor, Laurie, 127
Leal, Ann Haywood, 146
Leatherdale, Mary Beth, 96
The LEGO Neighborhood Book (Lyles), 137
L'Engle, Madeleine, 30, 160
Leonardo and the Renaissance (Horris), 159
Leonardo da Vinci, ix, 156–162
Leonardo da Vinci (Corsi), 159
Leonardo da Vinci (Lafferty), 160
Leonardo da Vinci (Marshall), 160
Leonardo da Vinci (Mason), 160
Leonardo da Vinci (McLanathan), 160
Leonardo da Vinci (Provenson), 161
Leonardo da Vinci (Raboff), 161
Leonardo da Vinci (Romei), 161
Leonardo da Vinci (Tracy), 162
*Leonardo da Vinci and the Renaissance in
      World History* (Lassieur), 162
"A Lesson from Frank," 153–155
Let It Shine (Pinkney), 107
Let Women Vote! (Brill), 61
"Let's Read Short Shorts," 35–38
LeVine, Harry, 132–133
Levinson, Nancy Smiler, 62
Levitin, Sonia, 60
Lewis, J. Patrick, 108
Liftoff (Mitchell), 124
Lily and Dunkin (Gephart), 150
Lin, Maya, 103, 137, 140
Lisa, Bright and Dark (Neufeld), 144
Lisle, Janet Taylor, 71, 146

Littlesugar, Amy, 105
A Long Way to Go (Oneal), 60
Look at That Building (Ritchie), 137
Looking for Alaska (Green), 201–202
Lord of the Deep (Salisbury), 77–78, 80–81
Loving, Richard and Mildred, 109–110,
      113–114, 166–167
Loving v. Virginia, 109–114, 167
Lowry, Lois, 36, 43, 71, 83, 95, 147, 178,
      179
Lucretia Mott (Bryant), 61
Lyles, Brian and Jason, 137

M

Macaulay, David, 136
Maccarone, Grace, 164
MacLachlan, Patricia, 22, 32
Madeline (Bemelmans), 21, 44
Making a Difference (Hodges), 62
"The Man in the Moon," 121–124
Manhattan Project, 128–133
The Manhattan Project (Elish), 133
Margaret and the Moon (Robbins), 127
Mariposa Blues (Koertge), 18
marriage
      interracial, 109–114, 166–167
      problems in, 7–8, 10
      same-sex, 4, 109, 113–114, 167
Marshall, Norman V., 160
Marsico, Katie, 69
Martin, Ann M., 36
Mason, Antony, 160
Masterpiece Mix (Munro), 162
Matthews, L. S., 95
Maudie and Me and the Dirty Book (Miles),
      182
Maya Lin (Harvey), 140
Maya Lin (Langmead), 137
Mazer, Harry, 71
McCully, Emily Arnold, 60, 110, 126,
      164
McLanathan, Richard, 160
McLaurin, Charles, 99, 100, 103
Meltzer, Milton, 160, 183
Memoirs of a Bookbat (Lasky), 181
mental illness, 142–143, 144–150
Mercado, Nancy E., 36
Meyer, Carolyn, 182
Meyers, Madeleine, 61
The Mighty Miss Malone (Curtis), 5
Miles, Betty, 182
A Million Shades of Gray (Kadohata), 46

Miss Lina's Ballerinas and the Wicked Wish (Maccarone), 164
Missing May (Rylant), 14, 22
Mississippi, civil rights and, 97–108
The "Mississippi Burning" Civil Rights Murder Conspiracy Trial (Fireside), 107
Mister Doctor (Cohen-Janca), 93
Mitchell, Don, 106, 124
Mixed Me! (Diggs), 111
Mommy Laid an Egg! (Cole), 197, 199
Mona Lisa, 156–161
Monk, Isabell, 111
Monroe, Judy, 183
Montgomery, Lucy Maud, 21, 44
More More More, Said the Baby (Williams), 111–112
Morrison, Taylor, 160
Mother Jones (Kraft), 62
Mott, Lucretia, 56, 61–62
Moulton, Erin E., 146
"Moving Day," 49–51
Mr. Ferris and His Wheel (Davis), 137
Muhlberger, Richard, 160–161
Munro, Roxie, 162
Murder in Mississippi (Currie), 107
Museum of Jewish Heritage, 86–87
musicians, 166–168
My Mom's Having a Baby! (Butler), 193–194, 197
"My Mother Was Rosie the Riveter," 125–127
My Two Grannies (Benjamin), 112
Myers, Walter Dean, 16–20, 32, 33, 154

N

National Coalition against Censorship, 175, 178–179, 202
Naylor, Phyllis Reynolds, 4, 173, 178, 186–192, 205
Nazario, Sonia, 32
Nazis, 71, 84, 92–93, 94–96
Nest (Ehrlich), 14, 143, 147
Neufeld, John, 144
New Paths to Power (Smith), 63
New York Times v. United States (Herda), 183
Nineteenth Amendment, 50, 57, 59, 61, 63, 69
The Ninja Librarians (Downey), 184
"No One Wanted Us," 94–96
Nobel Prize, 167–168
Nolan, Han, 146
nonfiction books, blog on, 131

nonfiction series, 148
Number the Stars (Lowry), 71, 83, 95

O

O'Brien, John, 168
O'Connor, Jim, 168
Odhiambo, Eucabeth A., 143
Office for Intellectual Freedom, 175, 178, 193, 202
Oh, Freedom! (King and Osborne), 107
Ohm, Deborah Gore, 61
"On the Street Where I Lived," 141–143
One Crazy Summer (Williams-Garcia), 4, 24, 27–34
One Word from Sophia (Averbeck), 112
Oneal, Zibby, 60
Opdyke, Irene Gut, 92
Oppenheimer, J. Robert, 128–130, 133
Orr, Tamra, 106
Osborne, Linda Barrett, 107
Osman, Karen, 161
The Other Half of My Heart (Frazier), 112
Outbreak! (Barnard), 142

P

Painting (Pekarik), 161
Painting (Waters and Harris), 161
parents
    book ratings for, 200–203
    relationships with, 16–20
Parker, Steve, 124
Pascoe, Elaine, 183
Past Perfect, Present Tense (Peck), 37
Paterson, Katherine, 13, 22, 37, 95
Patron, Susan, 22, 32
Paulsen, Gary, 37
Peck, Richard, 37, 40, 182
Pekarik, Andrew, 161
Penguin Random House website, 69, 81
Philbrick, Rodman, 4, 33
Picture This (Woolf), 162
Pinkney, Andrea Davis, 95, 107, 164
plagues, 64–69, 142–143
"Playing House," 3–5
Polacco, Patricia, 4, 111, 114
political campaigns, 115–117
The Printer's Apprentice (Krensky), 181
Prisoners of the Empire series, 72–81
Provenson, Alice and Martin, 161
P.S. Be Eleven (Williams-Garcia), 24–27, 29–31, 34

Q

The Question of Miracles (Arnold), 6–15

R

Rabble Starkey (Lowry), 147
Raboff, Ernest, 161
Race to the Moon (Parker), 124
racism, 28, 76, 103, 105, 167. *See also* civil
    rights movement
Radical Red (Duffy), 60
Rappaport, Doreen, 62, 183–184
ratings, book, 180, 200–203
reading
    exploring the world through, 44–46
    joy of, 39–40
reading levels, 41–43
"Reading Turquoise," 41–43
The Rebellious Alphabet (Diaz), 181
Reed, M. K., 184
Refugee (Gratz), 96
refugees, 92, 94–96
Reich, Susanna, 168
Reid, Constance Bowman, 126
Remember the Ladies (Johnson), 62
Renaissance, 156–162
The Renaissance (Wood), 162
rescue operations, 85–93
research
    authors' process of, 65–66, 75–76,
        86–89, 99–101, 129
    for students, 59, 158, 178–179
Revolution (Wiles), 105
rights, civil, 97–108, 109, 113–114, 131,
    167
rights, First Amendment, 173–174,
    175–185. *See also* intellectual freedom
right-to-die issues, 7, 9, 15
Ritchie, Scot, 137
The Road to Paris (Grimes), 112
Robbins, Dean, 127
Roberts v. U.S. Jaycees (Gold), 61
Rocky Road (Kent), 147
Romei, Francesca, 161
Romer, R. M., 93
Rosie the Riveter, 50, 125–127
Rubel, David, 62–63
Rubin, Susan Goldman, 84, 93, 97–104,
    108, 138, 155
Rylant, Cynthia, 14, 22

S

Sacred (Arnold), 9, 11, 13

The Safest Lie (Cerrito), 85–93
Salinger, J. D., 171
Salisbury, Graham, 71, 72–81
Saltz, Gail, 196
same-sex marriage, 4, 109, 113–114, 167
San Francisco, 64–69, 136
Save Halloween! (Tolan), 182
Scary Stories to Tell in the Dark (Schwartz),
    178
Scattergood, Augusta, 105
Scherer, Glenn, 133
Schmidt, Gary D., 18
*Scholastic Encyclopedia of Women in the
    United States* (Keenan), 62
Schwartz, Alvin, 175, 178
science, gender gap in, 126
science books, 123–124, 126–127, 128–134,
    135–140, 142–143
Scieszka, Jon, 37
The Search for Belle Prater (White), 32–33
The Second Mrs. Giaconda (Konigsburg),
    ix–x, 156–158
The Secret Garden (Burnett), 22, 142
The Secret of the Manhattan Project
    (Gonzales), 133
The Secret Project (Winter), 134
Selma and the Voting Rights Act (Aretha),
    107–108
Sendler, Irena, 86–93, 104
series nonfiction, 148
sex and sexuality, 193–199
Shadow of a Bull (Wojciechowska), 45
Sheinkin, Steve, 128–134
Shelf Life (Paulsen), 37
She's Wearing a Dead Bird on Her Head!
    (Lasky), 60
Shh! We're Writing the Constitution (Fritz),
    53, 116
Shiloh (Naylor), 173, 178, 205
short stories, 35–38
Shusterman, Neal, 18
"Sidetracked by Books," 39–40
Silhouetted by the Blue (Jones), 147
similes, 34
Singer, Marilyn, 164
Skira-Venturi, Rosabianca, 161
Sky Boys (Hopkinson), 137
Sky High (Zullo), 137–138
Skyscraper (Curlee), 138
Slacks and Calluses (Reid), 126
Small Acts of Amazing Courage (Whelan), 46
Small as an Elephant (Jacobson), 147

Smile like a Plastic Daisy (Levitin), 60
Smith, Karen Manners, 63
Snyder, Laurell, 165
So B. It. (Weeks), 147
Somewhere in the Darkness (Myers), 16–20, 33
songs, by Bob Dylan, 166–168
Sons from Afar (Voigt), 18
The SOS File (Byars), 37
Soto, Gary, 35–36
space exploration, 121–124, 127
A Splash of Red (Bryant), 155
Stanborough, Rebecca, 136
Stand Up and Sing (Reich), 168
Stanley, Jerry, 63
Stanton, Elizabeth Cady, 50, 52–53, 55–62
Steele, Philip, 184
Stehlik, Tania Duprey, 112–113
Steins, Richard, 184
Stone, Tanya Lee, 123, 126
Stormy Seas (Leatherdale), 96
Strasser, Todd, 36, 134
Streatfeild, Noel, 163
Student Nonviolent Coordinating Committee (SNCC), 98, 107
students
    activities for, 15, 20, 34, 58, 113–114, 131–132, 139–140, 178–179
    anecdotes about, 153–155
    behavior of, 82–84, 121–123
    discussion questions for, 19–20, 33–34, 57–58, 148–149, 158, 179–180
    research for, 59, 158, 178–179
"Studying the First Amendment," 175–185
suffrage movement, 55–63, 69
Sullivan, Edward T., 133
Sullivan, George, 63
Super Women (Lawlor), 127
Sure Signs of Crazy (Harrington), 5, 147
Survivors (Zullo and Bovsun), 37, 83
Survivors Club (Bornstein and Holinstat), 84
Swan (Snyder), 165
Sway (Turner), 33
Syrian refugees, 95–96

T
Tailfeather, Speck Lee, 135
Take a Look (Davidson), 159
Tales from Outer Suburbia (Tan), 38
"Talking with Angela Cerrito," 85–93
"Talking with Dori Hillestad Butler," 193–199
"Talking with Elana K. Arnold," 6–15
"Talking with Gennifer Choldenko," 64–69
"Talking with Graham Salisbury," 72–81
"Talking with Rita Williams-Garcia," 24–34
"Talking with Steve Sheinkin," 128–134
"Talking with Susan Goldman Rubin," 97–108
Tallulah's Solo (Singer), 164
Tan, Shaun, 38
Taylor-Butler, Christine, 185
Terrible Typhoid Mary (Bartoletti), 83, 143
Their Lives in Their Words (Rappaport), 62
There Goes the Neighborhood (Rubin), 138
There's Going to Be a Baby (Burningham), 197–198
"They Laughed," 82–84
The Thing about Jellyfish (Benjamin), 14
This Bridge Will Not Be Gray (Eggers), 138
Thompson, Julian F., 182
Thor, Annika, 95, 203
"Three Bombs, Two Lips, and a Martini Glass," 200–203
The Three Little Pigs (Guarnaccia), 138, 139
"The Times They Are a-Changin" (Dylan), 166–168
Tinker vs. Des Moines (Rappaport), 183–184
Tolan, Stephanie S., 182
Tomecek, Stephen M., 136
Tracy, Kathleen, 162
travel, 44–46
Treviño, Elizabeth Borton de, 45
The Trials of Molly Sheldon (Thompson), 182
"Trouble, Folks," 115–117
The Trouble with Mothers (Facklam), 181
True Colors (Kinsey-Warnock), 33
The Truth about Truman School (Butler), 195
Turner, Amber McRee, 33
Twelve Impossible Things before Breakfast (Yolen), 38

U
The Ultimate Weapon (Sullivan), 133
Under 18 (Kronenwetter), 183
Under the Blood-Red Sun (Salisbury), 71, 72–81
The United States in the 20th Century (Rubel), 62–63
Uschan, Michael V., 107

V
Van Allsburg, Chris, 36–37
Van Dusen, Chris, 136–137

Vaughan, Marcia, 93
Vaught, Susan, 144–146, 148–149
Ventura, Piero, 161
Violet (Stehlik), 112–113
Viva, Frank, 139
Voigt, Cynthia, 18
voting
    citizenship and, 115–117
    rights to, 50–51, 55–63, 69, 102–103,
       106–107

W

Waiting for Filippo (Bender), 159
Wallmark, Laurie, 127
war, 70–71, 72–81, 85–93, 125–127
Warner, Gertrude, 22
Waters, Elizabeth, 161
The Watsons Go to Birmingham—1963
    (Curtis), 14, 205
We Shall Not Be Moved (Dash), 61
We the People (Faber), 182
websites
    "Alice" series, 189–190
    Holiday House, 38, 93, 108
    on interracial marriage, 113
    Penguin Random House, 69, 81
The Wednesday Wars (Schmidt), 18
A Weekend with Leonardo da Vinci (Skira-
    Venturi), 161
Weeks, Sarah, 147
What Daddy Did (Shusterman), 18
What I Heard (Geller), 19
What Makes a Leonardo a Leonardo?
    (Muhlberger), 160–161
What's Inside Your Tummy, Mommy?
    (Cocovini), 198
What's the Big Idea, Ben Franklin? (Fritz), 53
Whelan, Gloria, 46, 96
When Thunder Comes (Lewis), 108
When You Were Inside Mommy (Cole), 198
Where Willy Went (Allan), 198
Where's the Ballerina? (Claybourne), 165
White, Ruth, 32
Who Built That? (Cornille), 138
Who Has What? (Harris), 198

Who Is Bob Dylan? (O'Connor and O'Brien),
    168
Who Was Frank Lloyd Wright? (Labrecque),
    139
The Whole Story of Half a Girl (Hiranandani),
    147
Wilde, Oscar, 180
Wiles, Deborah, 105
Williams, Vera B., 111–112
Williams-Garcia, Rita, 4, 24–34
Winstanley, Nicola, 111
Winter, Jonah, 134
Wojciechowska, Maia, 45
Wolf Rider (Avi), 19
women
    rights of, 50–51, 55–63, 69
    during World War II, 125–127
Women's History Month, 49–51
Women's Right to Vote (Marsico), 69
Wood, Tim, 162
Woods, Brenda, 110
Woolf, Felicity, 162
The World of Daughter McGuire (Wyeth), 113
World War II, 70–71, 72–81, 85–93,
    125–127
Wright, Susan, 106
Wyeth, Sharon Dennis, 113

Y

The Year of the Bomb (Kidd), 132
Yep, Laurence, 69
Yolen, Jane, 38
You Want Women to Vote, Lizzie Stanton?
    (Fritz), 53, 55–59
Young Frank, Architect (Viva), 139
Yousafzai, Malala, 96

Z

Zane and the Hurricane (Philbrick), 4, 33
Zeinert, Karen, 184
Zindel, Paul, 132, 178
Zuehlke, Jeffrey, 136
Zullo, Allan, 37, 83
Zullo, Germano, 137–138
Zusak, Markus, 84, 203